John Davidson's guide to
Walking and Cycling in Inverness and the Highlands

50 routes for locals and visitors

Published in 2011 by
Tread Wisely Publications
17 Stratherrick Gardens
Inverness, IV2 4LX
www.treadwiselypublications.com

Printed in Scotland by J Thomson Colour Printers

ISBN # 978-0-9565999-0-2

A catalogue record for this book is
available from the British Library

Route maps are based on 1920s Ordnance
Survey 1" Popular Edition, purchased in electronic
form from the National Library of Scotland.

Highlands overview map in introduction © Maps in Minutes 2010.

The author and publisher have made every effort to ensure the
information and route descriptions provided here are a true and
accurate reflection. However, we cannot be held liable for your
safety whilst following these routes. You must take responsibility
for your own actions and undertake any of the routes knowing
your own abilities and limitations.

John Davidson's guide to
Walking and Cycling in Inverness and the Highlands

50 routes for locals and visitors

TREAD WISELY
PUBLICATIONS

■ Walking through the woods at Dores

WALKS

■ Cycling on the Great Glen Way

CYCLES

Introduction

Wide open spaces, magnificent mountains, glorious glens and quiet roads make the Highlands and islands a fantastic place to enjoy the great outdoors.

From Inverness – the capital of the Highlands – you can explore a range of landscapes, wildlife and human influence, all within easy reach.

Getting out and about to research this collection of superb walking and cycling routes, I have discovered wonderful areas, intriguing history and met some fascinating people.

I've ventured to Durness in the far north-west corner of Britain, gone over the sea – or at least the bridge – to Skye, found myself in some of the remotest glens in Scotland, and climbed some testing mountains.

But I've also had some fine outings starting right on my doorstep.

For me, that is the beauty of Scotland and the Highlands in particular – this vast area is accessible to all, or at least to those who venture out and seek it.

I hope these 50 routes will be an inspiration to you, whether you hope to experience them all or just a few.

The book is not a collection of the best routes in the area (though many of them could surely claim to be), but a personal choice of some of the many routes I have enjoyed during my time so far in the north of Scotland.

There's enough in this one small book for a lifetime of adventures in the Highlands, yet this is only a taste of what is out there.

The routes range from simple family strolls to adrenaline-pumped expeditions.

This guide aims to give the information required to plan your trip yourself, deciding which route is suitable for you and making sure you have the proper equipment and experience where necessary.

Many of the routes venture into remote parts and it is vital to have the skills to navigate and look after yourself where there may be no mobile phone or GPS coverage.

In my rucksack

Each of us has our own way of packing for an adventure in the outdoors, but some things are a must.

Waterproofs and warm clothes definitely fall into this category, whatever the time of year. I shove a hat and gloves in the sack, even in summer, and take spares in the winter, as well as an extra fleece.

I always tend to wear my 3 to 4 season walking boots wherever I'm heading, whether it's climbing a Munro or wandering around Inverness.

However, when I'm on the bike I tend to just wear trainers, and I rely on my waterproof socks to keep out the worst of the weather.

Food and drink is another essential, and I would always carry more than I expected to need, especially when heading to the hills or into more remote areas.

On a number of the routes, refreshments can be few and

■ Bikes hiding behind a tree near the Allt Garbh in Glen Affric (left)

▶

■ The Culloden Viaduct

▶ far between, so self-reliance is the key.

I also carry at least one map along with my compass wherever I am, even if I think I know the route well.

Other bits that tend to live in a compartment of my rucksack are a whistle for emergencies; a head torch; some gaffer tape to fix anything; my penknife; fully charged mobile phone; basic bike tools and spare inner tube; a first aid kit; and – for the sake of luxury – a sit mat.

Well, a dry bum can make all the difference!

In winter some of the mountain routes in particular require specialist equipment and the knowledge and experience of how to use them. At such heights, snow or ice can last for many months of the year.

Using this book

The routes in this book have all been tried and tested by myself, and I have given a clear indication of what to expect on each outing.

Each one has a brief summary, with some details outlined.

The distance is given in miles, and this, along with the surface summary and route details, should give enough information to help plan your own trip.

I have purposely not given a time, as this depends on so many variables, not least the experience and fitness of those involved.

All the routes require you to have some basic map reading skills, and I have suggested what I believe is the best map or maps for that particular walk or cycle.

I have also noted where particular navigation skills are required, especially on mountain routes or over pathless terrain.

This note means these routes are serious outings and experience is essential – they are not to be taken lightly.

The Ben Wyvis epic, for example (Walk 8), is a very long and tiring outing, and I did that one in the long daylight hours of summer in clear conditions. It would be a huge undertaking in inclement weather as the ridges and tracks are not well defined.

Similarly, the Across Ross route (Cycle 17) is a real challenge and requires some serious stamina. It's a route you should build up your skills and experience before trying.

The main thing is to know what you are capable of. This book

contains routes for every level of walker and cyclist, so you must decide what is suitable for your own abilities.

Maps

I have a passion for maps and, for me, their beauty often lies in their simplicity.

The maps I have drawn alongside each route are intended only as a sketch map – they are not to scale and should not be used for navigation purposes.

There are some wonderful maps available for this purpose, and I have noted what I believe is the most appropriate one for each route in the route summaries.

The main ones are the Ordnance Survey Explorer and Landranger series; Harvey maps – which are designed specifically for outdoor enthusiasts; and Trailmaps, which are produced locally by Steve Smirthwaite in Nairn. These are available from a number of large

and small outlets in the Highlands or from his website at www.trailmaps.biz, while the OS and Harvey maps are widely available in outdoor stores and book shops.

National Cycle Network

Many of the cycle routes in this book use part of the National Cycle Network – and in some cases follow it religiously.

The NCN covers more than 12,000 miles across the UK and around Inverness it offers great opportunities to explore north, south, east and... not west as yet, though a route to Fort William is on the cards.

The NCN links Inverness to Glasgow, Edinburgh, Dundee, Aberdeen, Perth, Tain and even John o'Groats.

It uses mainly minor or B roads in this area, with some traffic-free cycle path sections.

The network is organised by a charity called Sustrans, though responsibility for the route lies with individual landowners and local ▶

► authorities. You can find out more about the work of Sustrans at www.sustrans.org.uk or by calling 0845 113 00 65.

Route developments

By their very nature, some routes can change. While I don't expect too many roads in the Highlands to be torn up in the near future (after all, some of them are still in the same place they are on my 1920s maps), land use can affect paths and tracks, particularly in remote areas.

Forestry work can have a big influence, particularly when large areas are cleared, which could potentially distort some of the descriptions in this book. Please follow requests from land managers if any of these routes are affected by such works.

Other changes can have a much more positive effect, such as the plan to develop a National Cycle Network route between Inverness and Fort William.

There are also discussions taking place at the time of writing about cycle routes between Dingwall and Strathpeffer and Inverness and Beauly, both of which could improve some of the routes in this book.

Bike shops & repairs

Whether you want to hire a bike, stock up on spares or get some repairs done, there are plenty of bike shops in the areas covered in this book.

I've given the details of some

■ A mountain biking marker post in Daviot Wood (left) and me heading north en route to Durness with bike trailer in tow (right)

of the main ones here, so you can get on your way without too much delay:

Inverness

● Alpine Bikes – 2 Henderson Road, Inverness, 01463 729 171, www.alpinebikes.com/shops/tiso-inverness-outdoor-experience
● Bikes of Inverness – 39-41 Grant Street, Inverness, 01463 225 965, www.bikesofinverness.co.uk
● Halfords – Harbour Rd, Inverness, 01463 223 388, www.halfords.com
● Highland Bike Co – 38-40 Waterloo Place, Inverness, 01463 234 789, www.highlandbikes.com
● Monster Bike – 7 Canal Rd, Inverness, 01463 729 500, www.monsterbikeinverness.com
● Ticket to Ride Highlands – bike hire and transport – Cantraybruich Cottage, Culloden Moor, Inverness, 07902 242 301, www.tickettoridehighlands.co.uk

Nairn

● Bike n Buggy – Falconers Lane, Nairn, 01667 455 416, www.bikeandbuggy.co.uk

Dingwall

● Dryburgh Cycles – Tulloch Street, Dingwall, 01349 862 163, www.dryburghcycles.co.uk

Strathpeffer

● Square Wheels – The Square, Strathpeffer, Ross-Shire, 01997 421 000, squarewheels.cubecycles.co.uk

Access – rights and responsibilities

In Scotland we have some of the most open access laws in the world, making it the perfect place for outdoor enthusiasts like myself.
    Basically, the law allows you ▶

Enjoy Scotland's outdoors responsibly

Everyone has the right to be on most land and inland water providing they act responsibly. Your access rights and responsibilities are explained fully in the Scottish Outdoor Access Code.

Whether you're in the outdoors or managing the outdoors, the key things are to:

- **take responsibility for your own actions**
- **respect the interests of other people**
- **care for the environment.**

Visit **outdooraccess-scotland.com** or contact your local Scottish Natural Heritage office.

■ Athnamulloch bridge and Strawberry Cottage at the end of Loch Affric

▶ the right of responsible access onto most land and inland water. Your rights and responsibilities are set out in full in the Scottish Outdoor Access Code, which forms part of the Land Reform Act (Scotland) 2003.

The text below outlines the basic principles behind the code:

Enjoy Scotland's outdoors responsibly

Everyone has the right to be on most land and inland water for recreation, education and for going from place to place providing they act responsibly. These access rights and responsibilities are explained in the Scottish Outdoor Access Code. The key things are:

When you're in the outdoors:
● take personal responsibility for your own actions and act safely;
● respect people's privacy and peace of mind;
● help land managers and others to work safely and effectively;
● care for your environment and take your litter home;
● keep your dog under proper control;
● take extra care if you're organising an event or running a business.

If you're managing the outdoors:
● respect access rights;
● act reasonably when asking people to avoid land management operations;
● work with your local authority and other bodies to help integrate access and land management;
● respect rights of way and customary access.

Visit outdooraccess-scotland. com or contact your local Scottish Natural Heritage office.

SNH's Inverness office can be contacted on 01463 725 000 or recreationandaccess@snh.gov.uk

You can also contact Highland Council on access@highland.gov. uk or visit www.highland.gov. uk/leisureandtourism/what-

▶

► to-see/countrysideaccess for further information on access.

Being prepared

Going into the outdoors, it's best to be prepared for any conditions at all times of year.

However, taking time to check the weather forecasts is a great way to get an idea of whether you'll need your full waterproofs ready to grab at the top of the rucksack, or if you can stuff them at the bottom just in case.

● Met Office – www.metoffice.gov.uk
● Mountain Weather Information Service – www.mwis.org.uk
● BBC weather – www.bbc.co.uk/weather

I'd also recommend checking the avalanche service if you do decide to tackle any mountain routes in the winter, though again you should only do this if you have the appropriate skills and experience.

● Scottish Avalanche Information Service – www.sais.org.uk

Beasties

There is even a forecast for midge conditions in Scotland now! This is available at www.midgeforecast.co.uk

It's important to protect yourself against these biting beasties if you're out and about during the spring, summer and autumn.

Protective sprays are available which can help protect against midges and ticks, as well as other unruly insects. I always carry one in my rucksack and put some on before I head out, particularly round the ankles, sleeves and face/neck area.

When out in the wilds, you're especially vulnerable to bites. Ticks are the worst in the Highlands as they have the potential to carry lime disease, so it's important to check after a day out if any have attached themselves to you. If they have, you can remove them using a special remover or a pair of tweezers, but it's vital to remove the whole of the mouth part.

For more information on ticks, visit www.tickalert.org

Don't let this put you off enjoying the beautiful countryside in the Highlands – it's just good to be aware of what else is out there! ■

■ One of General Wade's military roads in the forests around Carrbridge (right)

Key to route maps

Stream/river/loch	Allt Garbh River Beauly Loch Ness
Railway (station)	Muir of Ord
Track	
Path	
Minor road	
Main road	B9006
Trunk road	A9
Route (direction)	
Campsite	Car park — Youth hostel
Bike route (NCN)	7
Bike repairs	Picnic area — Cafe

Highlands overview map

This map shows the main areas featured in this book, to allow you to picture the extent of the routes and how to reach them.

■ Ben Hope and the beautiful single-track road to Altnaharra (see Cycle 21)

Lochinver

Ullapool

Kinlochewe

Shieldaig

Portree

Broadford

Mallaig

Durness

Alltnaharra

Lairg

Tain

Alness

Strathpeffer

Nairn

INVERNESS

Cannich

Drumnadrochit

Fort Augustus

WALK 1

Explore the community-owned forest at Abriachan with this fine walk to a summit offering panoramic views

Start/finish Abriachan Forest Trust car park
Distance 4 miles
Surface Good paths and tracks throughout, some steps and steep sections
Map Abriachan Trailmap

Beyond the steep slopes rising up from the shores of Loch Ness, Carn na Leitire is a beautiful hill offering spectacular views across Inverness-shire.

It is a surprisingly low one, however, at less than 1500ft (434m) above sea level, and the Abriachan Forest Trust trails offer easy access to this wild area.

The car park is easily accessible by taking the Abriachan turn-off from the A82 south of Inverness and following signs to 'Forest Walks'.

The route begins by taking the easy access path behind a notice board at the far end of the car park, turning right in front of the Arc – just one of many interesting features which make this forest great fun for children and families to explore.

It has been owned by the local community since March 1998 when the trust bought 534 hectares to safeguard access and improve biodiversity, as well as create jobs.

Continuing round to the right you soon reach a replica Bronze Age round house. Turn left onto a good path – part of the popular cycle trails through the forest – then go left again onto a rougher path a few hundred metres on at a wooden marker post with a footprint graphic.

Soon there is a steep climb through deciduous woodland up to one of a number of interestingly carved benches. These are well-placed rest stops and it's lovely just to take your time and take in the views over Loch Laide and northwards towards

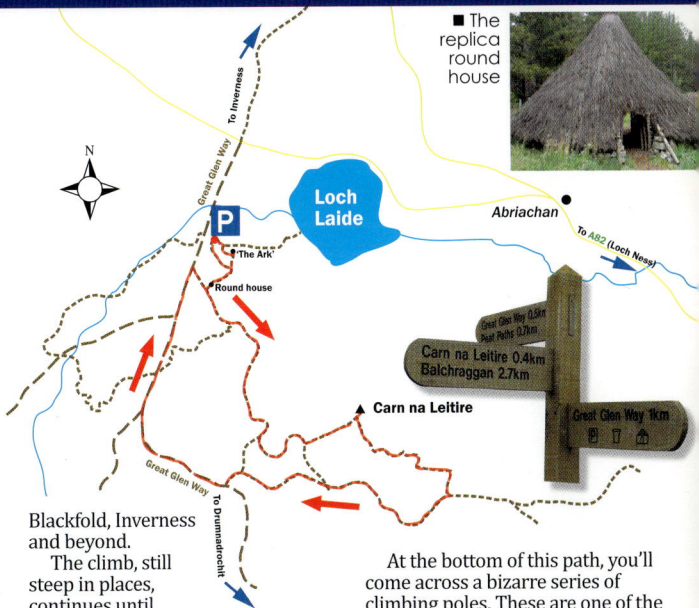

■ The replica round house

Loch Laide

Abriachan

To A82 (Loch Ness)

To Inverness

Great Glen Way

P

'The Ark'

Round house

Great Glen Way 0.5km
Peat Paths 0.7km

Carn na Leitire 0.4km
Balchraggan 2.7km

Great Glen Way 1km

■ Carn na Leitire

Great Glen Way

To Drumnadrochit

Blackfold, Inverness and beyond.

The climb, still steep in places, continues until you reach a wooden signpost which directs you left towards Carn na Leitire near another bench.

There is no mistaking the route to the summit now as a well-made path leads all the way to a cairn across open ground.

After enjoying the magnificent views, which take in the lochs and hills on the south side of Loch Ness, continue on the excellent path, which heads south-east through a peat bog, with occasional information panels full of intriguing information about the history of the area.

■ Clear paths lead to the summit cairn of Carn na Leitire (left)

At the bottom of this path, you'll come across a bizarre series of climbing poles. These are one of the fitness exercises on the Peat Path To Fitness, which you now join by turning right – the extra activities are purely optional, thankfully!

This route leads back into the trees and eventually drops to meet the Great Glen Way at a well signposted junction. Turn right towards Inverness and the Abriachan Forest Trust car park and follow the blue marker posts along the vehicle track.

Before the car park, turn right at a sign for Abriachan Forest Trust paths to return to the round house and find your way back through the easy access trails to the parking area, with its eco toilet, barbecue and children's play park.

WALK 2

Climb high above Loch Ness for wonderful views before following a return path along the shore of this famous loch

Start/finish Inverfarigaig Forest car park, just off the B852 at Inverfarigaig
Distance 6.5 miles
Surface Mostly on paths and tracks, some short road sections
Map OS Explorer 416

Take the high road and then the low to link up these two villages on the south shore of Loch Ness.

The circular route is varied, with nice woodland paths, a rocky summit, some lovely waterfalls and a shoreside track to experience on the way.

It begins at the nice little Forestry Commission car park at Inverfarigaig, initially following a wooden marker post on the Lochan Torr an Tuill Walk.

Follow the green markers until that route turns right a short way up the hill and instead continue straight on, meeting a track on the red route after a short but steep climb. Turn right onto the track and follow it to Boleskine.

Ignore a sign right to Foyers via Shore Path and go straight on up the track, which soon narrows to more of a path (boggy in places) which is followed through to a more open area of heather and shrub.

I love the narrow winding path which works its way through the undergrowth, forking right – still with the red markers – where another green route diverts left. It's a lovely spot and you soon cross a tiny burn on a plank before clambering up a steep slope back into a more mature fir forest.

Watch closely here for red arrows painted on trees and rocks which direct you to the top of Toman Tarsuinn, a 219m hill with fantastic views down to Loch Ness over the trees.

Keep following the markers to meet a vehicle track on a hairpin bend, and turn right to follow the track downhill until it meets the B852 road at a primary school. Go left on the road and head up the hill to a gate, where the Falls of Foyers are signed down into a wood on the right.

Go carefully down the sometimes steep slope – looking out for native red squirrels – towards Lower Foyers, emerging at a road near Foyers Bay House.

Turn left and walk to the end of the road, turn left and follow the road round, going left towards the metal bridge. Just before the bridge, take a path right to loop around the shore. After crossing the footbridge near a fish farm, go left along the road then take a path right at a blue post.

The climb here is to avoid the hydro-electric power station. Turn left onto the road and follow it beyond a house, going left at a sign to Inverfarigaig via Loch Shore.

There is a nice section through birch

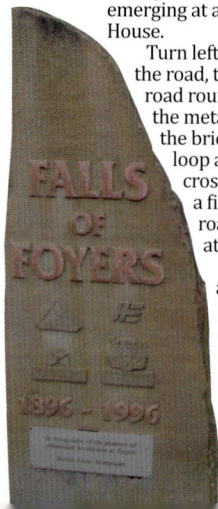

wood here which meets a tarmac track. Go right then left immediately behind a sub-station to pass below a pylon and join a path which soon leaves the industrial mess behind and becomes a tranquil route along the shore of Loch Ness.

Eventually you come to the old pier at Inverfarigaig and, standing on the now damaged structure, it feels like you are right out in the middle of this massive loch.

Continue up the tarmac track to the right, passing a few houses before reaching the main road 50 yards from the turn off to the car park at Inverfarigaig.

■ Marker posts direct you through the forest paths

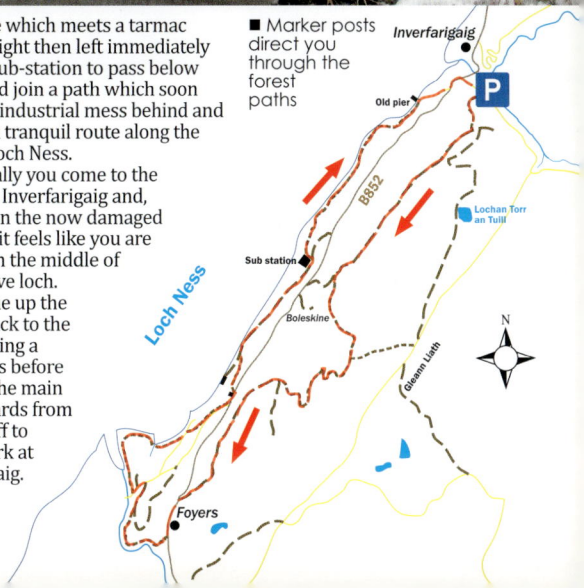

Inverfarigaig

Old pier

B852

P

Sub station

Loch Ness

Boleskine

Lochan Torr an Tuill

Gleann Liath

N

Foyers

WALK 3

An exciting walk along the edge of the Beauly Firth before climbing to an Iron Age fort

Start/finish Muirtown Locks, Canal Road, Inverness
Distance 5.5 miles
Surface Canal towpath, pavements, woodland trail, minor roads, some steep sections.
Map OS Explorer 416, Inverness Trailmap

This varied route takes in the 19th century Caledonian Canal, a local nature reserve and a woodland walk up to a fort believed to have been visited by St Columba in 580AD.

All this is within reach of Inverness city centre, and you can even reach the starting point on foot by following Greig Street and Fairfield Road up from the River Ness.

Otherwise there is car parking beside the canal bridge off Telford Street or on Canal Road, a left turn immediately after the bridge when travelling from the centre of town.

From the top lock, the walk begins by following the towpath down to the swing bridge on the city side of the canal. Cross the road and follow the canal path round the outside of the British Waterways marina alongside the deep Muirtown Basin.

Ignore a path leading right to South Kessock Old Pier (see Walk 16) through the Merkinch local nature reserve.

After another lock, cross the railway at a level crossing to follow it out to the sea lock, a cold place at the best of times! You are right out in the firth here and you can feel it.

The mountains at the far end of the Beauly Firth look different every time I am here, but always spectacular whether in clear air or shrouded in cloud.

Cross the seaweed-covered lock and head up the tarmac access road on the far side.

Follow the tarmac round to the right through Clachnaharry – a village which originally housed workers who built the canal – and go over a metal bridge over the railway. Turn right at the road and follow the pavement opposite until the traffic lights, where a path

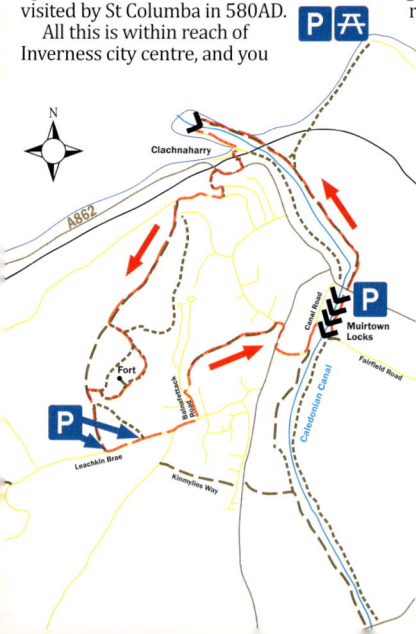

■ The signal box at Clachnaharry in evening sunlight

goes left up steps at a hole in the wall.

Keep left through the woods to emerge at the end of a cul-de-sac where you turn right and follow the steps directly ahead. Go right onto the minor road and follow it under dense tree cover to a green gate into the woods on your left.

This steep but beautiful path through conifer woodland is always a pleasure to walk and is the best spot in the Craig Phadrig forest to spot red squirrels.

At an open turning point, go left on the yellow markers. A short distance ahead, follow the blue marker and soon turn right to steeply climb towards the fort, which is best accessed just before this path begins to drop steeply, where a clearly eroded steep slope heads up to an oval-shaped clearing where the walls of the fort once stood.

The fort was a stronghold of the Pictish King Brude and it is believed to have been destroyed by fire in around 700AD.

Continue to follow the path down the steep hill and go left to follow the yellow markers to a car park. Go through the car park and left downhill on the road, keeping left on Leachkin Road then turn left onto Balnafettack Road.

After a short uphill stretch, turn right onto Kingsview Terrace and follow a nice little path past the end of the road that heads down through the Scorguie area of Inverness to come out behind Moray Firth Radio's office.

Turn right at the bottom then immediately right again onto King Brude Road. After 150 metres, turn left down Canal Road and follow it round a tight bend to return to the locks.

WALK 4

■ Nigg Hill from the Cromarty Sutors walk

Explore the history of the high cliffs above this beautiful old village

Start/finish Shore Street, Cromarty (follow signs to car park through village)
Distance 3.5 miles
Surface Earthy paths, steep in places with steps; minor roads.
Map OS Explorer 432

Standing guard at the entrance to the Cromarty Firth, the north and south sutors are gigantic cliffs that rise dramatically out of the sea.

They have offered a natural defence to the area, particularly during the two world wars when the firth provided a key safe haven for vessels in need of repair.

On this walk up the south sutor, above Cromarty, you will see solid evidence of the defensive role this picturesque area played during the wars.

Today, the views from the concrete lookouts are obscured by trees but between the branches you get a sight of the magnificent water below and, across the sea, the north sutor, dotted with caves at its base.

It's hard to imagine the scene up here in this peaceful place during those more turbulent times, but the ruined structures give us a reminder of the importance of this place.

Down at the village, the walk starts at a small car park at the end of Shore Street, which you reach by following the car park signs as you enter the village on the A832.

Follow the road past the old fish store, now a bright green building on the seafront, and along the coast to reach an old-style black signpost.

The sutors are signed left along Miller Road, which you follow to a corner, where a path leads off left at a low sign round the shore side of a house.

This is a delightful little path which keeps to the water's edge with the sutors ahead and Nigg Hill opposite. Here you pass the beach where geologist Hugh Miller spent much of his youth collecting fossils. There is a National Trust for Scotland museum in Cromarty

Cromarty Mains 1 Mile   **MacFarquhar's Bed** 1½ Mile

outlining his life and achievements, which also includes the thatched house where he used to live.

Soon the path begins to climb in amongst the trees and it gets steep in places, using steps and boardwalks built into the hill. Nearer the top, after passing the lookouts, you get a spectacular airy view over the water to Nigg Hill.

The path emerges at a small parking area at the end of a narrow road. Head right down this road, diverting left to the viewpoint, from which it is possible to see for miles across the Highlands.

Continue down the quiet road, which passes farmland and offers wonderful views back over the village to Easter Ross, Ben Wyvis and beyond.

Turn right at a crossroads to head down

the steep hill. The road swings past the old Cromarty House, with an interesting graveyard opposite, and down to meet the outward route at the end of Miller Road.

It's worth exploring the village while you're here. As well as the Hugh Miller Museum it also has a number of art and craft shops, the Cromarty Courthouse Museum and the East Church, amongst other attractions.

There's also a ferry operating between here and Nigg (see Cycle 22) where you can visit Nigg Old Church as part of the Highland Pictish Trail.

■ Looking back to Cromarty from the shore-side path

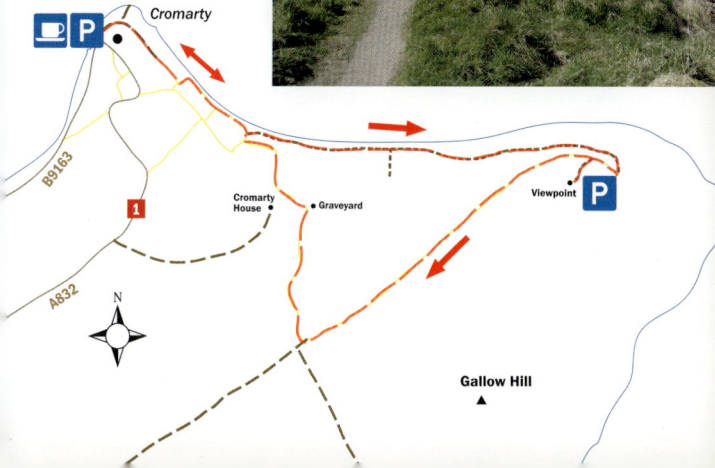

WALK 5

■ The once-grand Guisachan House

Discover a hidden water feature to rival its better known neighbour

Start/finish Plodda Falls car park (grid ref. NH279238)
Distance 3.5 miles
Surface Paths and tracks, steep in places
Map OS Explorer 415

The spectacular waterfall at Plodda is a must-see attraction for any visitor to the area but, if you're willing to explore a little further, there's another intriguing water feature in the area.

On the way to the car park, you'll have travelled directly above it without being able to get a glimpse.

Home Fall – or Guisachan Fall as it is called on the map – is a beautiful fanned waterfall with an interesting history.

But this walk starts with a visit to its impressive neighbour at Plodda, following the Forestry Commission signs to the new viewing platform which overlooks the falls from the top.

There used to be an iron bridge – originally built by Lord Tweedmouth in 1880 – over here but this had to be removed as it was too dangerous. Now you can peer over the 40-metre drop to the plunge pool below.

Continue downhill on the path and

■ Looking down from the top viewing platform at Plodda Falls

Plodda and Home Falls

take a left turn to get a spectacular view of the same falls from below. Once here, you get a sense of scale and you can also appreciate how much the platform you were just stood on overhangs at the top!

Retrace your steps back up this path then turn left to continue downhill on the green markers to a vehicle track at a wide ford in the Abhain Deabhag. I wouldn't advise trying to cross at this ford unless you're in a good old-fashioned 4x4!

Instead, turn right onto the track and ignore coloured markers off to the right to pass a couple of houses and then reach the ruins of Guisachan House, once a grand stately home by the looks of it.

Keep to the track round the back of the house and, once at the far side, look for a small grassy path opposite the house's south-east facing wall. This path keeps

right of the burn heading up to the falls, crossing a small estate fence.

A short distance upstream, this enticing little path crosses over fallen trees and under overgrown shrubs then, all of a sudden, you'll see the remains of an old iron fence.

Battling through the undergrowth, you very soon arrive at the beautiful Home Fall, as it is known locally.

Looking around, you'll notice the remains of another building and, if you look above to the right of the waterfall, a series of rusted iron rings. These used to guide a pipe down to the building, which housed a small-scale hydro-electric system that once powered the house at Guisachan.

Return to the track at Guisachan and turn left onto it to continue the circuit. Keep left at a fork and head towards a steep grassy bank ahead.

The track skirts right below the bank and passes through a patch of trees and shrubs to reach a fence.

Stay just inside the fence to the left and follow it past Hilton Lodge to meet the forest road.

Go right and follow it back to the car park.

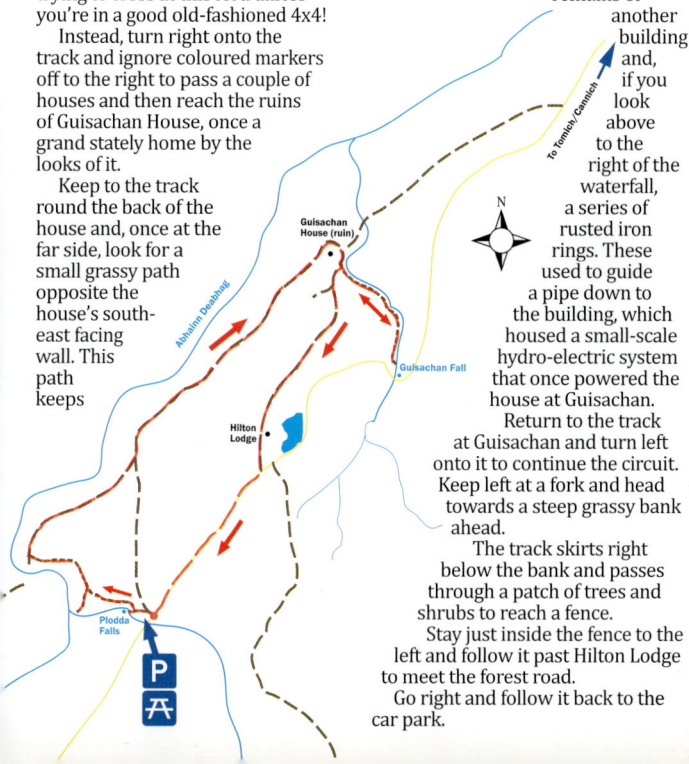

Abhainn Deabhag

Guisachan House (ruin)

To Tomich / Cannich

N

Guisachan Fall

Hilton Lodge

Plodda Falls

P

WALK 6

A varied walk exploring the west side of Inverness over a wooded peak

Start/finish Kinmylies shops, off General Booth Road, Inverness
Distance 6.5 miles
Surface Paths and vehicle tracks, boggy and wet sections; stretch on minor road; main road crossing
Map OS Explorer 416; Inverness Trailmap

Dunain Hill dominates views looking west from Inverness, with its three communications masts rising above the tree line, and it offers fine views in return from its summit.

From the start of this energetic walk in the residential area of Kinmylies, the route climbs 280 metres to the top of the hill before dropping down on beautiful paths to the Caledonian Canal for a flatter finish.

There is parking at Kinmylies behind the shops off General Booth Road or nearby at Charleston Community Complex.

From the shops, cross the road using the underpass and follow the pedestrian sign to Leachkin Road up a shared-use path that climbs steeply. On reaching the road, turn right then left up Leachkin Brae, passing forest walks at Craig Phadrig on your right.

The climb is relentless on this minor road but the views behind you are worth pausing for and are a great excuse for a breather! Just beyond a turning off to Blackpark the road levels and you soon turn right onto a vehicle track which continues for some distance to briefly meet the Great Glen Way at a pylon.

A short distance on, leave the Great Glen Way to go left past a heavily padlocked gate and climb up the track. Go left at the first main track

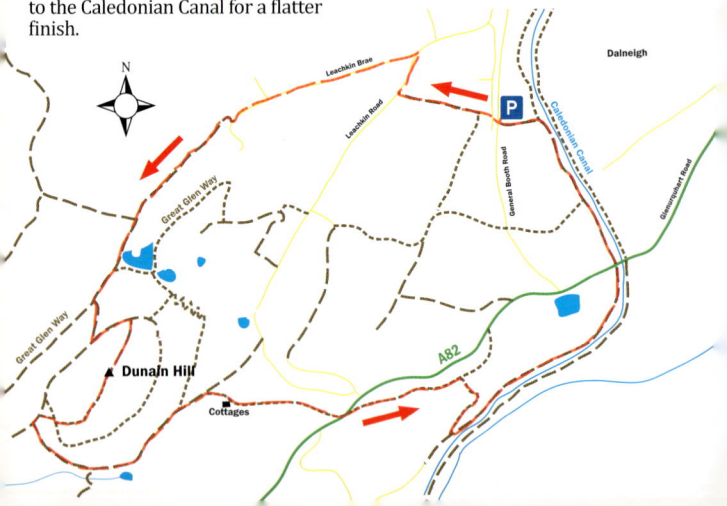

■ Dunain Hill with its communication masts visible from the Kessock Bridge across the city

junction then right at the second for the final steep push up to the summit of Dunain Hill, which lies a short distance beyond the masts at a very old looking cairn amongst the trees.

There is a nice viewpoint looking over Inverness if you head just left of the masts as you approach them.

The route continues through the middle of the masts onto a soggy path, used by walkers and adventurous mountain bikers. It's a tough test on two wheels but for walkers it leads nicely down the ridge of the hill.

Where the path levels and curves to the right, you meet a crossroads of paths. Go initially right then diagonally left and you'll soon meet a vehicle track. Turn left onto it then left again onto a less well defined track before the pylons, known locally as the "vomit track".

Having tried to run and cycle up this track, I understand where it gets its name, but this downward route is a nice walk which eventually curves to the left, crosses an old fence and levels out.

You emerge after a simple metal gate at the corner of a tarmac track, where you go diagonally down to the right, past the "No Through Road" sign. After the cottages, cross a stile made from a felled tree trunk and continue down this beautiful path right down to the main A82 road.

Cross carefully onto a track diagonally opposite, which leads behind the horses' field, squeezing past gorse bushes then onto a good path. Follow this to a fork, where a right turn leads you downhill to meet the Caledonian Canal after a steep final descent.

Turn left and follow the towpath back to the Tomnahurich Bridge and across the A82 again to continue, staying left of the canal, past the golf course and behind some football pitches. Turn left after the pitches to return to the Kinmylies shops.

See some of Britain's tallest trees in a historic forest on this circular route west of Inverness

Start/finish Old North Inn, Inchmore
Distance 5.5 miles
Surface Tarmac path, quiet country roads, earthy forest path
Map OS Landranger 26

Once home to Britain's tallest tree, Reelig Glen has lost none of its charm since losing the crown to a bigger rival.

It's an enchanting sort of forest and it owes this largely to a James Baillie Fraser (1783-1856), who imported and planted so many of the trees when the Reelig estate was owned by the Fraser family. They sold it to the Forestry Commission in 1949 and there is now a car park and a short walk with information panels along the way.

However, this slightly longer walk starts out at Inchmore on the B862 Inverness to Beauly road. There is a car park beside the Old North Inn where an information board outlines a number of interesting walks in the area.

I find this one a great evening stroll in the summer, with its magnificent views over the Beauly Firth, and it's also a nice distance – if a little hilly – for runners.

It starts by crossing the main road at the pelican crossing then turning right past a gallery onto a path, with a wooden signpost pointing to Reelig Glen. Keep on this path as it veers away from the roadside and meets a minor road on a corner.

Go straight ahead on this quiet

A nice path leads away from Inchmore towards the tall trees

Reelig Glen tall trees

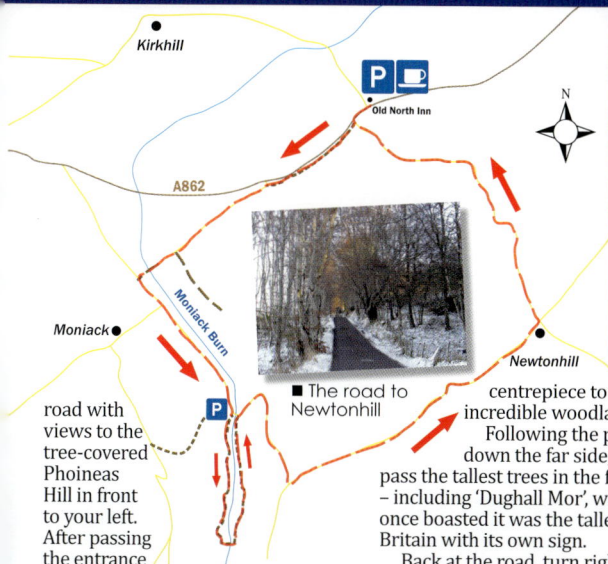

Kirkhill

Old North Inn

A862

Moniack Burn

Moniack

N

■ The road to Newtonhill

Newtonhill

road with views to the tree-covered Phoineas Hill in front to your left. After passing the entrance to Reelig House, the main residence of the estate, continue over the decaying bridge, now closed to traffic, and turn left onto another minor road.

Keep straight ahead towards Reelig Glen where the road swings round to the right and you soon come to the small car park.

Head straight through the car park and take a path at its far end to enter this wonderful glen, full of smells and sounds. Take a look at the information boards that tell you about the different species of trees along the way.

About a kilometre upstream, the path crosses a wooden bridge. From here you can see the overgrown remains of a beautiful arched bridge which would once have been the

centrepiece to this incredible woodland.

Following the path back down the far side, you pass the tallest trees in the forest – including 'Dughall Mor', which once boasted it was the tallest tree in Britain with its own sign.

Back at the road, turn right and follow it steeply uphill round a couple of sharp bends and up to a road junction where you turn left towards Newtonhill. It continues to climb for a while, though a little less harshly now.

A cleared area of forest on the left, as well as a number of crofts, opens up the views to your left over Kirkhill and the Beauly Firth to Ben Wyvis, particularly impressive in evening sunlight.

The road continues to a T-junction at Newtonhill, where you turn left to follow the road downhill back towards Inchmore. This is a great spot to see wildlife, from red squirrels and deer to buzzards.

You end up beside the gallery, where a right turn leads you back to the crossing and the inn.

WALK 8

■ Ben Wyvis from the long approach

Discover a more dramatic side to the Ben on this lengthy mountain trek

Start/finish Eileanach Lodge, Glen Glass, Evanton
Distance 17 miles
Surface Pathless mountain terrain, peatbog, ridges, river crossings, estate tracks, navigation skills required
Map OS Explorer 437

There's much more to Ben Wyvis than the flat-topped massif that can be seen from many parts of the Highlands.

Many of the routes in this book include a view of this magnificent mountain, though none of them are quite like you'll get on this close-up adventure.

On this side of the Ben, as it is affectionately called locally, there are corries, crags and cliffs that make it more deserving of its Munro status

– those Scottish mountains that reach more than 3,000ft above sea level.

Ignoring the popular approach to the summit from Garbat forest, off the A835, this route begins at the end of the Glen Glass road in Evanton, where there is space for a few cars at the turning point at Eileanach Lodge.

This is a long mountain walk, especially given the pathless terrain that makes it hard going for quite a way. But I feel you get to know the mountain better this way – and the views into Coire Mor furnish the Ben with a more spectacular reputation.

Head through the white gates at the end of the Glen Glass road and follow the track past the lodge, turning left ahead. Immediately beyond a ruined house, go right and pass through the gate. Follow the track out

■ The summit trig point and shelter on Ben Wyvis (left)

to the edge of the forest and onto the open hillside.

It's possible to cycle the first few miles, which might just save the legs later on!

The peaty track continues, fording the Allt Coire Misirich before rising to a small ridge just below Meall an t-Slugain Duibh. Leave the track now to head north over a small rise then go west up the protrusion called Leathad Dubh nan Iaron (marked on the OS 1:25,000 map only).

Once the ridge is gained, you get your first glimpse of the crags that rise up to Ben Wyvis from the rarely visited Coire Mor. The slabs and gullies here look superb in the sunlight, only adding to the charm of Ben Wyvis.

From the ridge, there is a clear, stony track that heads north-north-west to the 910m spot height. To visit the outlier Glas Leathad Beag, head east-north-east on grassy slopes to reach the small cairn.

Return to the 910m spot height

and traverse the grassy ridge towards Tom a' Choinnich. There are incredible views north and west on a clear day and it is possible to see from Torridon right round to Ben Hope in a stupefying panorama.

Descend from Tom a' Choinnich, initially south-east, following a vague path that dips south then climbs up to the highest point, Glas Leathad Mor. A trig point and shelter mark the summit of Ben Wyvis.

Continue along the ridge for another 500m or so then skirt left to follow a ridge above Coire na Feola. Soon after a defunct rusty gate, there is an emergency shelter and then a cairn, and the route down follows the line of the old fence.

Lower down, ford the Allt Coire na Feola then the more tricky Allt a' Choire Mhoir and continue to follow the fenceline along rough terrain. Once across the tributary Allt an t-Slugain Duibh, start to move above the main river and contour through the heather and peat to pick up the track near to where it fords the Allt Coire Misirich.

Follow the outward route back along the track to Eileanach Lodge, where you'll be glad to get your walking boots off at long last!

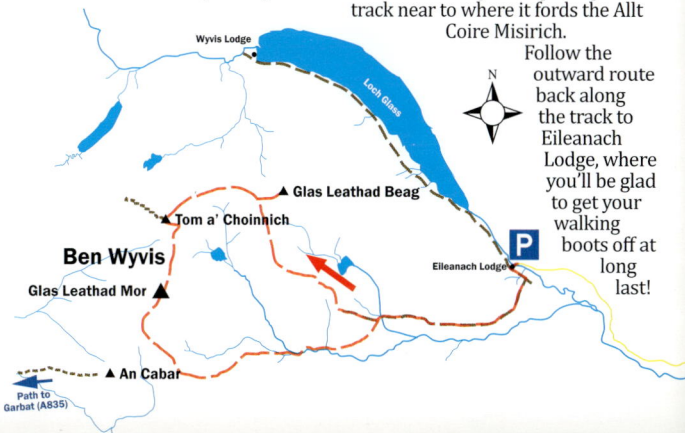

WALK 9

Explore this wonderful quiet area on the south side of Loch Ness

Start/finish Easterton, Loch Duntelchaig – grid ref NH632330
Distance 7.5 miles
Surface Forest tracks and paths, some very boggy; short sections on quiet single-track road
Map OS Explorer 416

A series of lochs, forests, hills and quiet roads make up the area to the south-east of Loch Ness. It's the perfect place to get away from the crowds and enjoy the peaceful surroundings of the Highlands just a stone's throw from the city of Inverness.

This walk is effectively two loops that could be done individually but together make a great outing between Easterton on Loch Duntelchaig and Bunachton, with the best view saved

until last. To reach the start, follow the B862 Dores road south from the city centre and turn left following a sign for Essich, Lochardil and Drummond. Go straight on at the Essich roundabout and continue to a crossroads near Loch Ashie. Turn left and follow the road until 25 yards after the second cattle grid, immediately before Easterton, where you can park at a large opening to a forest track on the left-hand side of the road.

You might notice a Rights of Way sign a short way down the road but the walk begins on the higher track, heading through the gate and into the forest.

Ignore a track off to

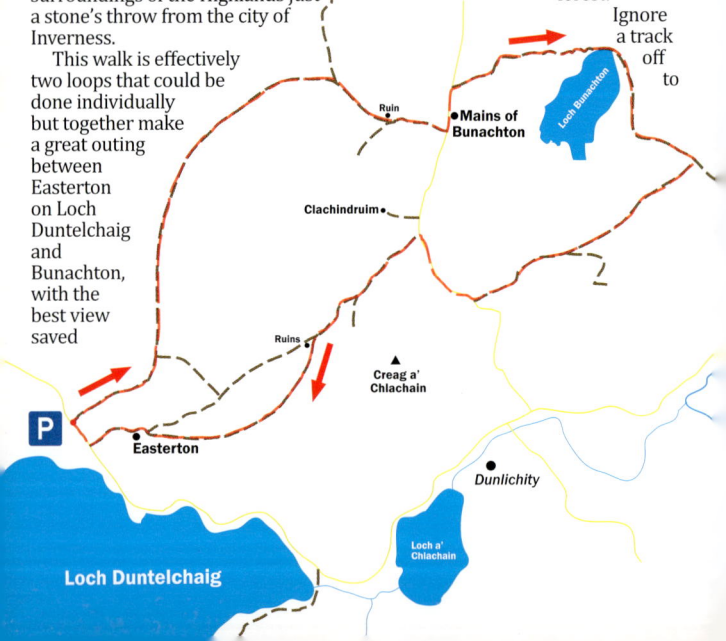

■ Glorious view of Loch Duntelchaig from Easterton

the right after half a kilometre and continue on the main track through the pine trees, where you might well see deer as you listen to the birdlife in the trees.

Keep right at a fork and eventually reach a gate at the end of the forest. Go through it and continue on the less obvious but straight track through overgrown gorse to a ruin beside a vehicle track. Go left in front of the old house and follow the track to meet the road.

Turn left and follow it past Mains of Bunachton then turn right onto a soggy farm track well before the plantation ahead. Go through the gate and cut diagonally to the corner of the trees, where the track goes through another gate to follow the edge of the forest (over an electric fence at one point) to finally drop to the shore of Loch Bunachton.

There's a fabulous view across the water here before you continue on a great little path up

into the trees and over the Gask Burn. You then turn right and follow a clear forest track all the way to the road.

Going right along the road you get a stunning view to the right through a clearing of the whole of Loch Bunachton.

Approaching a house, look out for a track off to the left just before a right-hand bend, where a sign points to Duntelchaig through the gate. Ignore a first track which forks left but further ahead go left of some ruins to follow a narrower but pretty tree-lined path all the way to Easterton.

At the house, go through a gate, keeping the house to your left, and follow the track right. From here you get the best view of the route – out across the largest of the south Loch Ness lochs, Duntelchaig.

Keep to the track to meet the road at the Rights of Way sign, and turn right to follow the road a short distance back to the start.

◄ Bunachton

WALK 10

Climb from a beautiful village to a monument in the hills overlooking Glen Affric

Start/finish Tomich Hotel
Distance 5 miles
Surface Forest tracks and paths, boggy, hill tracks, steep in places
Map OS Explorer 415

The attractive village of Tomich is situated on the old route into Glen

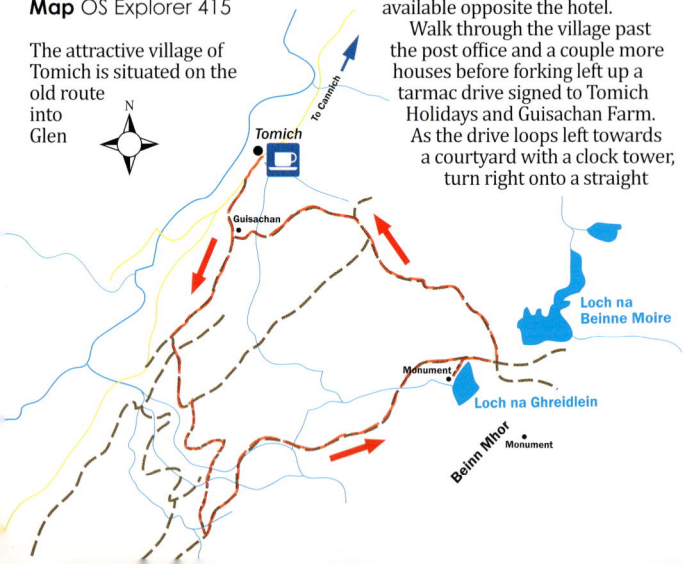

Affric and is worth a visit itself.

This walk climbs through a beautiful forest to a magnificent viewpoint taking in some of the spectacular Affric Munros.

It begins at the hotel in the village, 3½ miles from Cannich down a single-track road (see Cycle 14). There is some roadside parking available opposite the hotel.

Walk through the village past the post office and a couple more houses before forking left up a tarmac drive signed to Tomich Holidays and Guisachan Farm. As the drive loops left towards a courtyard with a clock tower, turn right onto a straight

Tomich monument

■ Loch na Beinne Moire

track with grass down the middle. This pretty route is lined with hedges and trees and is full of wildlife. Continue into the forest then take a track left where an old Scottish Rights of Way Society sign (pictured) points to Glenmoriston, going straight on at a crossroads and up the hill.

As the track bends right just after a hairpin left turn, look out for a small wooden post marking a path off to your right. A red arrow on the post points into the forest – this is the continuation of the Glenmoriston route – known locally as Eve's Road, which you follow.

A wonderful path goes among the trees and soon bends up to the left to follow the line of the Allt a' Bhuachaille, steeply in places and with a dramatic drop down to your right to the burn below.

At the top, go through a wooden gate onto the open hillside and follow the sign right to Glenmoriston, fording the burn before re-entering the forest through the nearby gate.

After a really muddy stretch, cross a few rickety boardwalks and, where the path gets a bit drier, turn left up the hill and over the brow before descending a great little path to cross a burn and head up the other side.

Go left at a path junction loosely marked by a thin wooden post. You'll soon get your first glimpse of the cross-shaped monument on top of Beinn Mhor as you reach the corner of a fence. Keep left of the fence for a short distance until a wooden gate leads out onto the open hillside.

Head under the electricity cables and follow the clearly defined – if wet – hill track, which follows the line of pylons for a short while before climbing high above them. Looking back now, the mountains of Glen Affric look fantastic on a clear day.

When Loch a' Ghreidlein comes into view to your right, you can follow a short track to detour to another monument near the boat house.

Continuing on the main track, you very soon get a fantastic view over Loch na Beinne Moire as you arrive at a crossroad of tracks. Turn left and follow the track downhill, under the line of pylons and beside a forest.

Go through a series of gates and swing right in front of a new house, keeping to the main track all the way as it bends left and emerges back at Guisachan Farm. Keep left round the courtyard to re-join the driveway back to the village.

WALK 11

Extend the viewpoint walk above Loch Ness to complete this nice circular route

Start/finish Allt na Criche forestry car park, 2 miles north of Fort Augustus off A82
Distance 6.5 miles
Surface Natural woodland path, steep in places; forest vehicle tracks; stony path; short tarmac section.
Map OS Landranger 34

Allt na Criche is a name you see repeated in many parts of the Highlands. That's because it translates as 'boundary burn', in this case between the old estates of Glenmoriston and Glenurquhart.

This walk begins by following the short viewpoint walk along the edge

of this boundary, before heading west to meet the Old Military Road that links Glenmoriston to Fort Augustus.

It gives fantastic views out over Loch Ness to Glen Roy and Glen Tarff – the line of the Corrieyairack Pass (see Cycle 20) – down to Fort Augustus and south to the mountains of the Great Glen.

The Forestry Commission car park is marked from the road, and the walk follows the large signpost at the back of it declaring 'Allt na Criche Walk'. Follow the beautiful path steeply up along the left edge of the burn, which you can hear tumbling down towards Loch Ness as you go.

You get a good glimpse at the peat-coloured water after crossing a small flat bridge over a tributary, then zig-zag up left away from the impressive little waterfall to meet a vehicle track.

Turn left to keep to the white markers and enjoy wonderful views to your left through the young trees to Loch Ness and beyond.

Ignore the next white marker, which leads left down into the woods again, and continue up to the right, staying on the track for another 2 miles through the woodland, then open heath and heather before a final stretch through mature conifers.

All the way along here, you can enjoy the rumble of water as a succession of burns plummet down the hillside to enter Loch Ness.

At a crossroad of tracks just before the Allt na Fearna, turn left. You are now on General Wade's Old Military Road, though much of it here has been turned into modern forest track.

If you look carefully, however,

■ The old military road leading uphill from the crossroad of tracks (left)

there are one or two signs of the original route, and I've found remains of culverts and bridges still just about visible through the dense undergrowth down here.

Where the new forest track turns sharply right, don't be tempted to follow this modern route! Instead, keep straight ahead through a soggy patch which soon turns into a reasonable path with a small bridge over a burn ahead.

The path descends steeply now, offering great views down into the village of Fort Augustus and the busy Caledonian Canal before zig-zagging down to meet another track. Go left and soon go through a gate onto a road at Jenkins Park.

Keep ahead along the road and turn left just after a playpark to follow the blue Great Glen Way markers. Look out for the one pointing left

■ Fort Augustus and the Caledonian Canal from the steep descent

just before a nice stone bridge on the road, and follow the path left up – steeply again – through the woods.

At the top, go right and follow the track past a viewpoint with a bench, where the white route you ignored earlier meets the track too. Continue downhill to a gate leading into the Allt na Criche car park.

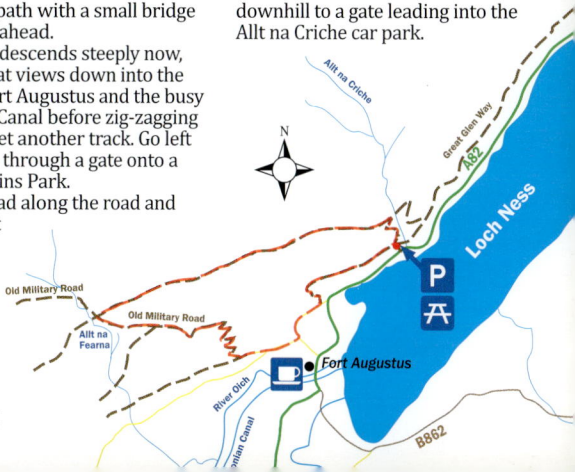

■ Walking along the path from Camasunary, with the Cuillin ridge behind

A wild walk on Skye with excellent views of the Cuillins

Start/finish Layby near Kilmarie on Broadford to Elgol road
Distance 10 miles
Surface Rough track, narrow cliff-top path, single-track road, vehicle tracks, cows in some open areas.
Map OS Explorer 411

Magnificent views of the Cuillin peaks and a dramatic cliff-top walk are among the attractions on this wonderful walk on the Isle of Skye.

It's tough going in places but the impressive surroundings more than make up for any extra effort you need to put in – plus, there's always the option of cutting it short once you get to Elgol if you can arrange transport.

The starting point is a few miles before the village at the end of the road just beyond Kilmarie.

Park on the left and follow the track opposite, signed to Camasunary. Already you can glimpse the tops of some of the Cuillin mountains jutting out into the skyline.

The rough and stony track, built by the army in 1968 to aid access for anglers to the loch at Coruisk, is hard going underfoot for walkers but makes the route easy to follow.

It leads up to a cairn then higher to the summit itself, from where there are stunning views ahead to the Cuillin ridge and, below, to the green fields of Camasunary.

Keep to the track as it descends sharply and turns left, giving views across the water to Rum and Canna. Go left across the boggy lowland when you reach a footbridge going the other way across the Abhainn nan Leac.

The path is indistinct and wet in parts but is continuous and therefore fairly straightforward to follow as it rises to climb

Camas Fhionnairigh Sligeachan
Camasunary 2.4m, Sligeachan 9.5m
Scottish Rights of Way and Access Society, Edinburgh

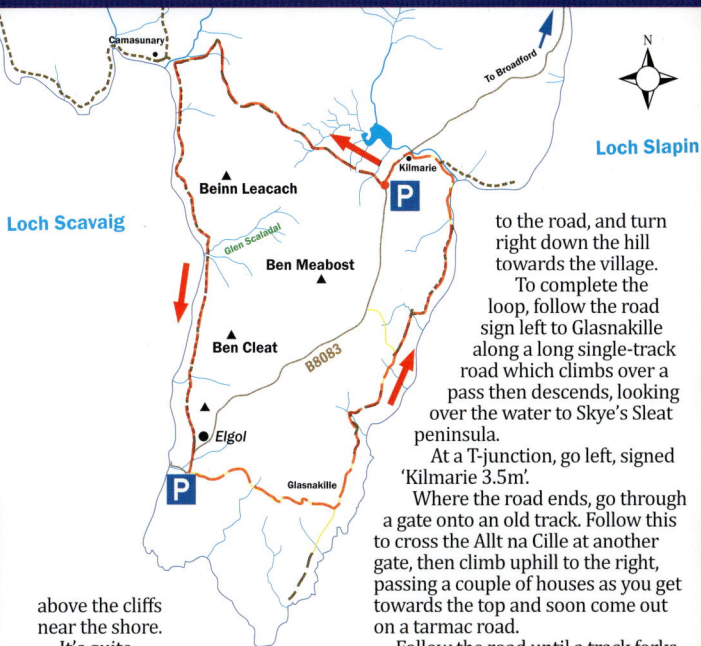

Loch Slapin

Loch Scavaig

Camasunary

Beinn Leacach

Kilmarie

Glen Scaladal

Ben Meabost

Ben Cleat

B8083

Elgol

Glasnakille

To Broadford

N

above the cliffs near the shore.

It's quite precipitous in parts, so keep a close eye on the path, even when your attention is caught by looking ahead to Soay, Rum and Eigg. The walking isn't difficult but you have to duck under a few overgrown trees here and there, and negotiate a couple of steep steps down before you reach the bay at Cladach a' Ghlinne.

Beyond Glen Scaladal, you climb back above the cliffs on another narrow path before eventually emerging at a fence on the outskirts of Elgol. Go through a gate and between fences on a narrow path

to the road, and turn right down the hill towards the village.

To complete the loop, follow the road sign left to Glasnakille along a long single-track road which climbs over a pass then descends, looking over the water to Skye's Sleat peninsula.

At a T-junction, go left, signed 'Kilmarie 3.5m'.

Where the road ends, go through a gate onto an old track. Follow this to cross the Allt na Cille at another gate, then climb uphill to the right, passing a couple of houses as you get towards the top and soon come out on a tarmac road.

Follow the road until a track forks off right and the road swings left. Take the track to go through a make-shift gate towards a house, then turn right where a stone helpfully marked 'path' directs you.

There's a great view of Bla Bheinn as you head along here through an area of ruins and through an old metal gate. Beyond another house the track improves and you meet the road beside the woods.

Stick to the road now as it skirts round the beautiful bay, past a historic burial ground and Kilmarie House to meet the main road. Turn left onto it to reach the car park.

WALK 13

■ Ridge leading up to Knockfarrel from Dingwall

Climb up the Cat's Back to enjoy a purr-fect stroll in Strathpeffer

Start/finish Blackmuir Wood, Strathpeffer
Distance 4.5 miles
Surface Forest tracks, woodland paths, boggy in places, steep, pavement
Map Trailmap Strathpeffer, Highland 5, Map5; OS Explorer 437

Knockfarrel is a great little hill offering panoramic views from its summit, where the remains of an old fort can be found.

This walk also passes through an old stone maze and follows part of the now defunct railway line, which used to bring the great and the good to the spa town of Strathpeffer in Victorian times.

The station platform is still there and you can imagine the steam trains arriving with the well-to-do tourists. The village remains popular with visitors today, and for very good reason.

There's plenty to see and do, including excellent cycling and walking.

This route starts at the Forestry Commission car park at Blackmuir Wood, at the west edge of the village. Follow the main track up through the woods and head through a gate after some houses.

Much of the forest has been cleared here and a path soon leaves the track left to head towards the Touchstone Maze. This structure, built in 1990, is made up of concentric circles of rocks from across Scotland.

The path winds its way uphill from the maze to emerge on a forest vehicle track, where you turn left onto the blue route. At another blue marker post, fork right off the track to go uphill quite steeply on a wonderful little path through birch trees.

This brings you out at a crossroads of paths on the ridge between Knockfarrel and Cnoc Mor, from which there are wonderful views below to Loch Ussie. Turn left over the stile to follow the delightful ridge in the direction of Knockbain and Dingwall.

As the way ahead drops steeply, aim for a small parking area on the line of the ridge and continue beyond it to the summit of Knockfarrel. The remains of an Iron Age vitrified fort can be made out under your feet as you take in the panoramic views from this exceptional viewpoint.

Return to the small parking area and fork right down a track, then soon take a small grassy path off to the right at a birch tree, leading you down to a signpost beside a Scots pine.

Turn right here and cross the stile to head steeply down a dead straight path between the fields. You can see the top of Ben Wyvis hiding

away behind the foothills as you drop down the hillside.

Go left over a wooden plank bridge and follow the top of a field until a gate, where the path cuts diagonally right to descend through some bog lower down. Cross the fence and go left, now on the line of the old railway.

The line was opened in 1885, when it took just 16 hours from London Euston – those were the days! It closed in 1951 and there are plans afoot now to turn it into a dedicated cycle and pedestrian route.

Stay left when you reach the end of the line and cross the wooden bridge onto the platform, where there are shops, a museum and a cafe. Head left of the station building up to the road and turn left.

There are plenty of shops, restaurants and cafes in the village centre to enjoy as you make your way back to Blackmuir Wood.

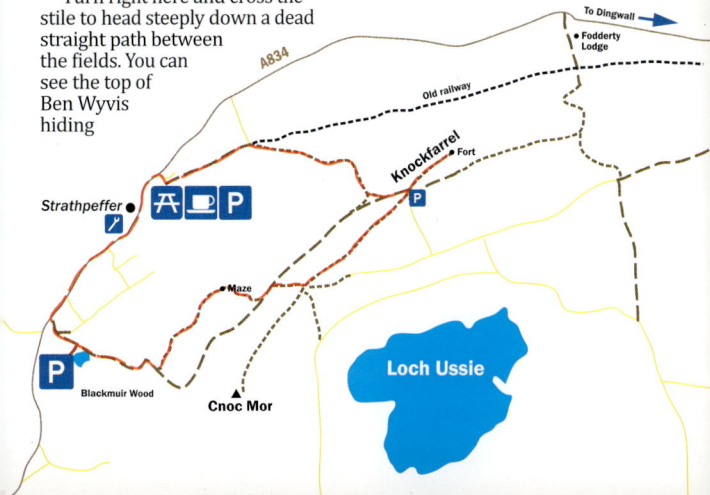

WALK 14

A trek around Culloden Muir that includes more than just the battlefield

Start/finish Culloden Battlefield Visitor Centre
Distance 5 miles
Surface Well-made paths, forest tracks, boggy in places, some road walking
Map OS Explorer 416

The site of the last battle to be fought on British soil is an eerie place. The visitor centre, run by the National Trust for Scotland, tells the fascinating story of the government's quashing of the Jacobite rising, known as the '45.

This walk begins there and takes a circuitous walk through the nearby Culloden Woods, visiting the creepy Prisoners Stone, where a number of Jacobite prisoners were shot in the aftermath of the battle on 16th April, 1746.

There's a charge for entry to the visitor centre, but you don't have to pay to walk through the battlefield itself. Go just to the right of the visitor centre and walk under a wooden walkway.

Take the left fork where the path splits in two then go right down the government line – marked by red flags – and turn left towards the large memorial cairn. Here you pass the graves of many clansmen and you are asked to be quiet in this area as it is a war grave.

Continue past the cairn and go straight ahead at a crossroads on the Jacobite line – marked by the blue flags – towards a metal gate. Go past the gate and turn left onto a tarmac access road. This leads straight ahead but the walk soon forks right after a large agricultural shed to join a grassy track into the woods.

A cleared area offers

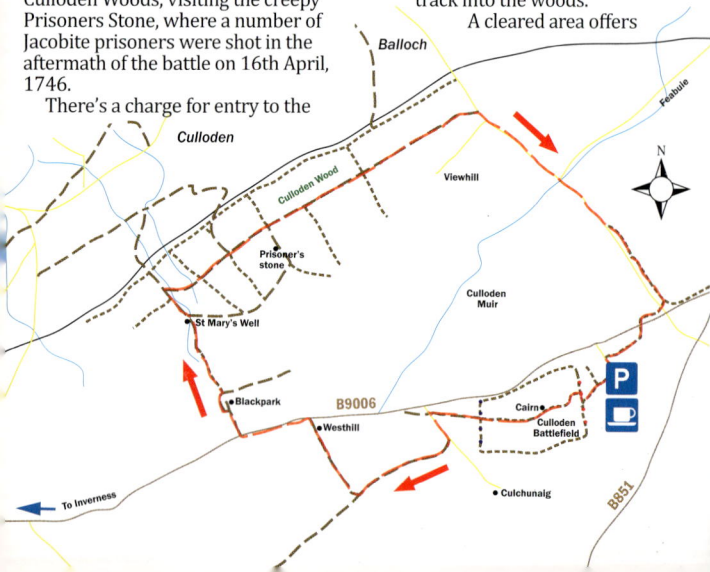

Culloden's bloody moor

fantastic views to the right across the Moray Firth to Ben Wyvis. Turn right down an unmarked track in the clearing which heads towards some houses. Duck under the gate at the bottom to pass the houses as you continue down the track to meet the B9006.

Go left and walk along the wide grassy verge on the left-hand side of the road until you see the sign for Blackpark Farm on the opposite side. Cross the road here and go down the farm's access track, going left before reaching the farm house to follow a parallel track where a small pedestrian sign directs you.

As the track bends to the right, a wooden sign points left to Culloden Wood. Follow this route down a boggy path between fields and go through the gate at the bottom into the woods, keeping to the track going straight ahead.

This leads through St Mary's Well, a 'cloutie well' where people go each spring to hang rags from the surrounding trees in a bid to bring them good fortune. This natural spring is said to be haunted by ghosts from the Battle of Culloden.

Go straight ahead after the well, then turn right at a crossroads a short way ahead. Follow this track for some way now, detouring right by the sign to the Prisoners Stone, which lies a few hundred yards off the main track.

Returning to the main track, continue along it, passing the school of forestry and heading out to the Balloch road, where you turn right and go past Viewhill. There is no path on this next section, so you must walk along the side of the minor road, which sometimes carries quite fast traffic. You can join a better verge on the left half a kilometre on at a horse riding sign, which leads to an excellent path beyond the entrance to the stables.

Follow this behind the trees to near the junction, then turn right towards the battlefield and cross the Balloch road, then the B9006 to take an old road right past a gate which leads back to the visitor centre.

WALK 15

Climb to a prominent summit above Loch Ness for a great view of the Great Glen

Start/finish End of minor road from Drumnadrochit to Grotaig
Distance 6 miles return
Surface Woodland paths; eroded mountain path through heather and rocks, boggy in places; high stile to cross.
Map Harvey Great Glen Way

You can't miss Meall Fuar-mhonaidh in views down the Great Glen. It's the highest point on the north edge of Loch Ness, and that makes it an excellent viewpoint.

From the top you can see for miles, all the way down the Great Glen over Loch Oich and Loch Lochy, and northwards to Dores and even out to the Moray Firth.

The Glen Affric and Kintail mountains make a spectacular backdrop to the west, with the village of Foyers and the distant Monadhliath mountains to the east, while the green fields above Drumnadrochit can be seen nearer to hand.

A minor road leaves the A82 as you pass through Lewiston at Drumnadrochit, signposted to Bunloit, Grotaig and the 'Pottery'.

The walk starts at a car park at the end of this single-track road, which climbs very steeply at first round a number of hairpin bends.

Watch out for pedestrians and cyclists along here, as this road is part of the Great Glen Way long-distance route.

Navigation on the route itself is fairly straightforward, although the summit lies 699 metres above sea level, so I'd advise taking a compass in case the potentially confusing top is shrouded in cloud.

A sign directs you from the edge of the car park to the 'hill footpath' along the continuation of the road, then right through a small gate beside

a bridge. The path at first follows the nice little Grotaig Burn then goes through a birch wood as it crosses a vehicle track before climbing up to the open hillside.

Your goal – the top – is never far from view but it rises impressively above the heather as you emerge from the trees.

The path is clearly eroded ahead as it climbs to a deer fence, which you don't catch sight of until you are upon it. Cross the high stile, where an old sign warns you about deer stalking, which takes place here between the end of August and mid-February. It won't affect this walk, however, as it simply asks you to stick to the track during this time.

That's exactly what you do now, following the eroded line through the heather and rocks up to the ridge and along to the summit.

It's a good hill climb, with some steep sections and a few boggy areas to negotiate, but there's also plenty of good sized rocks to stop and sit on, from which you can enjoy the views ahead.

The views are even better on the way down, as the hard work is done and you can see Loch Ness stretch out ahead of you as you return north to cross the stile and head back through the woods on the outward route.

As you approach the top, the first cairn you reach is a false summit – the track dips then rises beyond it to the summit plateau, where there are three more cairns. The highest point is the one furthest away, over to your right.

Hill Footpath

Great Glen Cycle Route

■ A sign near the car park directs you to the hill footpath, with the Great Glen Way (and its former cycle route) going left

■ Meall Fuar-mhonaidh from the path beside the Grotaig Burn (left)

WALK 16

See the sights on this flat walk
around the city's landmarks
and green spaces

Start/finish Town House, Bridge
Street, Inverness
Distance 6 miles
Surface Pavement, canal
towpath, earth paths
Map OS Explorer 416, Inverness
Trailmap

■ Picnic area
near old pier

If you really want to get a feel for
Inverness, this walk is the place
to start. It takes in the best of
both worlds – from man-made
monuments to the natural wonders
of this beautiful city.

Walking along, you seem to get a
new view around every corner. What
better way to explore the Highland
capital?

The route starts at the Town
House, next door to the Visitor
Information Centre in the heart of
the city. This building's main claim
to fame is that it housed the only
Cabinet meeting of the British
Government to be held outside
London, in September 1921, when
then Prime Minister David Lloyd
George was on holiday at Gairloch
in Wester Ross.

Walk away from the river and
turn right onto Castle Street
behind the Town House. Turn
right at the traffic lights beside
the castle onto View Place.

Follow the road downhill
before turning right down a
couple of steps to pass right of
Ness Bank Church and reach
the riverside, where you turn left
upstream. Across the water you
can see the beautiful cathedral
and, next door, the more modern
Eden Court Theatre. To detour to
these buildings, cross the river by
the pedestrian suspension bridge.

Otherwise, continue past the war
memorial onto Ladies Walk and

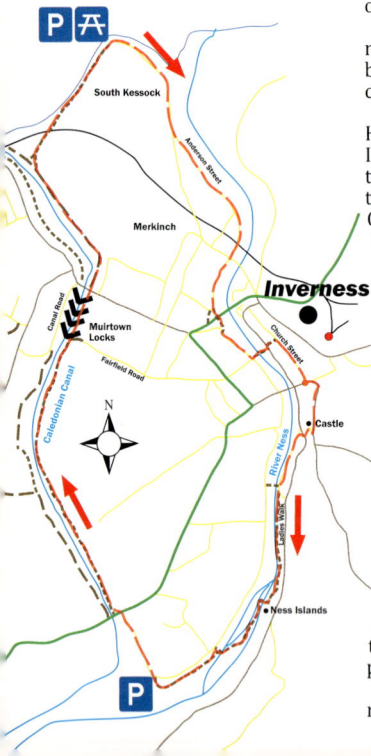

soon turn right over a pretty wooden bridge to Ness Islands.

These islands are a lovely spot in the city and are great for walkers, runners and cyclists. Follow the blue Great Glen Way markers through the islands until you reach the far side of the River Ness, where you turn left onto a tarmac riverside path.

Keep on this path until you reach a car park at Whin Park, then follow the GGW markers right. A path goes behind a wall the other side of the road, then through the leisure centre car park and out to the main road beside the Tomnahurich canal bridge.

Cross the road to join the towpath, keeping on the right-hand side of the canal to the Muirtown Locks about a mile further on.

Follow the series of lock gates down to emerge by another road swing bridge, where you cross straight over, and keep right of the black fence around the marina.

Go through a gate on a left-hand bend and follow the track along by the picturesque Muirtown Basin until shortly before the next lock gate, where a green pedestrian sign points right to 'Old Ferry Pier 1km'. Follow this path through the Merkinch Local Nature Reserve, which crosses the railway line then goes dead straight along the top of a sea wall with magnificent views out to the Black Isle and Ben Wyvis, as well as down

the Beauly Firth to the Strathfarrar hills.

The atmosphere is different here every time I visit, depending on the tides and the weather. It can be quite dramatic when the tide is high and the cloud is building over the distant mountains, while the mud flats at low tide are packed with wading birds searching for food.

There's a nice picnic area at the old pier, where the ferry used to cross the firth to North Kessock until the Kessock Bridge was built in 1982. Turning right, the view of the bridge is superb as you follow the road inland.

Take a quick signposted detour left to visit Carnac Point, at the dramatic mouth of the River Ness, before continuing up the road and forking left onto Anderson Street just before a shop.

Beyond Gael Marina and some new flats, follow the road to its end at the Black Bridge, then cross the road and follow the riverside under the Friars Bridge and up to the pedestrian bridge.

Go left to cross the river here and cross at the lights at the far side, going straight up Church Lane. Turn right at the top onto Church Street, passing Inverness's oldest house.

Abertarff House, built in 1593, is set back slightly from the other buildings on the street, which leads directly back to Bridge Street opposite the Town House.

■ Ness Islands marker post

■ Beinn a' Bha'ach Ard
as seen from Redcastle
on a calm winter day

**A tough hillwalking outing
that rewards with stunning
panoramic views and a
delightful ridge**

Start/finish Inchmore car park,
Glen Strathfarrar
Distance 10 miles
Surface Private tarmac road,
vehicle tracks, rough and
boggy in places, pathless
mountain terrain, navigation
skills required
Map OS Explorer 431

Seen from the Kessock Bridge across
the Beauly Firth, the prominent point
of Beinn a' Bha'ach Ard dominates the
view to the west.

It guards the entrance to Glen
Strathfarrar, a beautiful and peaceful
place, particularly as the number of
vehicles allowed down the single-
track road is restricted by the estate.
That makes it a wonderful place for
walkers and cyclists to explore.

This tough mountain walk is not
as straightforward as it looks from
back on the bridge, however. At 862m
(2828ft) Beinn a' Bha'ach Ard may

only be a Corbett, but it punches
above its weight when it comes to a
day on the hills.

For experienced hillwalkers, it is
a relatively short day – it takes me
around 6 hours to do this circuit – but
it covers a lot of pathless, heathery
ground on some significant slopes.

The reward is a magnificent view
from the summit, which takes in the
Cromarty and Beauly firths, as well
as a panorama of mountain tops. You
can tell why it's so clearly visible from
the Kessock Bridge when you're up
here looking down on what appears
to be a tiny bridge.

The walk starts at a small parking
area a short way down the minor
road to Glen Strathfarrar, signed off
the A831 Beauly to Cannich road at
Struy.

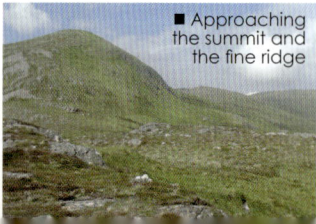

■ Approaching
the summit and
the fine ridge

Walk through the gate which restricts vehicle access (walkers and cyclists have access at any time) and continue down the road a couple of kilometres to the Culligran Power Station. Here, turn right onto a track which turns back on itself left and continues through nice birch wood.

Keep left at a fork to stay on the more obvious track until it passes under the pylons and reaches a dam on the Neaty Burn. The track deteriorates from here to a muddy mess as it swings right to follow the burn upstream and eventually onto the hillside.

Stick with the track until the ground starts to level off a little, then aim north-east for a lower top (marked 660m on the OS Explorer map) and, after a big dip, head towards the ridge proper around the 774m mark at Creag a' Gharbh-Choire.

It's tough going all the way up here and it doesn't ease until you can rest at the summit trig point and hopefully enjoy the fine

views, weather permitting.

Follow the delightful ridge round to Sgurr a' Phollain, from where it is possible to pick up the remnants of an old stalkers' path steeply down then along to meet a line of old fence posts at a small cairn.

Go roughly south-east from here, intermittently picking up the old path where you can, to descend to Loch na Beiste – being careful to avoid a gorge to the left near the bottom.

Cross at the head of the loch, pausing for the stunning views back up to the summit, and follow the now clear path down to meet a large gate.

Go through it and cross the burn, following a track through the field – where red deer stags are sometimes kept during the rutting season. The track roughly follows the line of the fence to your left down to another gate in the bottom corner of the enclosure, then continues as a better vehicle track down to leave the enclosure completely just above some houses at Inchmore.

Follow the track down to the right to meet the road opposite the car park.

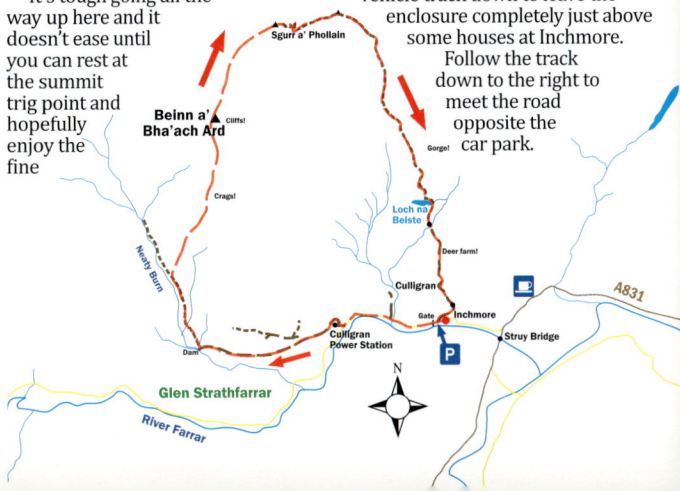

WALK 18

Follow the line of a dismantled railway to reach a popular dolphin-spotting point

Start/finish Station Hotel, Avoch
Distance 7.5 miles
Surface Earthy paths, tarmac, grassy path, beach
Map OS Explorer 432

Chanonry Point on the Black Isle is perhaps the best place on the British mainland from which to watch dolphins.
    This route combines two local walks, one heading down a grassy shoreline to the point from Fortrose and one along the old railway line between Avoch – pronounced with a silent "Av" – and Fortrose.
    The railway branch line, opened in 1894, once ran from Muir of Ord to Fortrose, bringing jobs and industry to the peninsula, but it closed to passengers in 1951 and for goods in

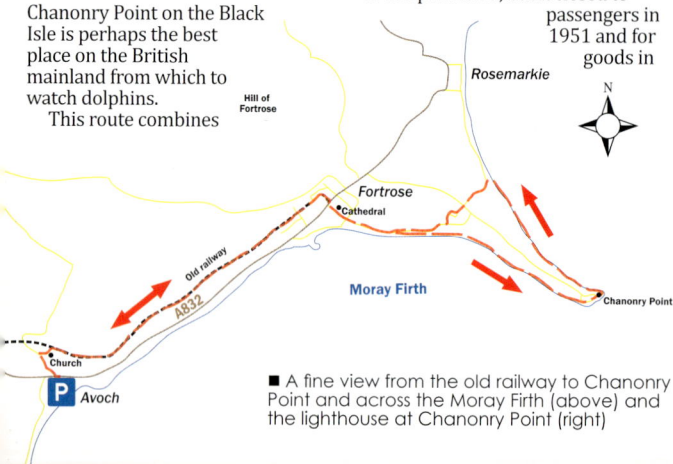

■ A fine view from the old railway to Chanonry Point and across the Moray Firth (above) and the lighthouse at Chanonry Point (right)

1960, along with many other lines throughout Britain.

The stretch of dismantled railway between Avoch and Fortrose now provides a vital link for walkers and cyclists, as the main road between the two villages has no pavement and is a very narrow, busy route.

The walk starts by following the road opposite the Station Hotel, beyond which there is a small car park signed from the main road. Go uphill to the church, turning right onto Braehead and following a wooden sign through the church car park to Fortrose.

Look out for surviving remnants of the old railway as you head along the obvious route, catching tantalising glimpses down through the trees to the Moray Firth.

Once you emerge at houses in Fortrose, follow signs to the village centre and you should reach the main road at Tavern Lane. Turn right then left in front of a restaurant, passing the 13th century Fortrose Cathedral.

At a picnic area, leave the road to take a narrow grassy path between hedges and keep as close as possible to the shore through the campsite. Then keep to the boundary of the golf course all the way to the lighthouse at Chanonry Point.

Look out for dolphins from the beach as you head round the point and follow the beach up the far side.

A shortcut back to Fortrose is signed from the edge of the beach in front of the golf clubhouse. At the T-junction, a small path opposite leads between gardens pointing to the Western Links.

You rejoin the outward route near the cathedral in Fortrose, from where you can return by the same route.

WALK 19

Climb to a high fort above Loch Ness as you explore two ancient woodlands

Start/finish Visitor Information Centre, Drumnadrochit
Distance 4.5 miles
Surface Mostly earthy forest paths, start on tarmac pavement
Map Harvey Great Glen Way

Taking in two local woods, there is plenty to see on this lovely woodland walk from the Loch Ness-side village of Drumnadrochit.

You will enjoy viewpoints overlooking Glen Urquhart and Loch Ness as you meander along some great little paths through these established forests.

From the car park at the Visitor Information Centre, turn right along the main road then take the first right up Pitkerrald Road, following pedestrian signs to Craig Monie and Balmacaan Woods.

The path soon heads off behind a giant redwood tree – and it is a true giant – where marker posts lead you off to the right on the combined red and green route.

Keep right on the lower path at an unmarked split to follow the red route, then stay right at a more obvious fork to follow the green route through Craig Monie woods.

This path undulates around the edge of the wood, where there is a chance to see red squirrels, until it swings upwards to the left. At the top, there is a viewpoint which looks back

■ Walking near the fort at Craigmonie

Drumnadrochit woods

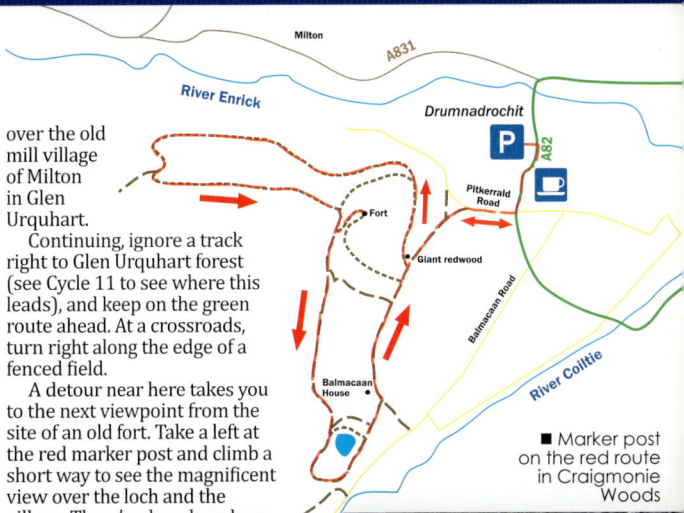

over the old mill village of Milton in Glen Urquhart.

Continuing, ignore a track right to Glen Urquhart forest (see Cycle 11 to see where this leads), and keep on the green route ahead. At a crossroads, turn right along the edge of a fenced field.

A detour near here takes you to the next viewpoint from the site of an old fort. Take a left at the red marker post and climb a short way to see the magnificent view over the loch and the village. There's a bench up here where you can relax and take it all in while you have a nice rest!

Return to the red marker by the same route and go left to continue along the circular route.

Keep nearest the fence as a number of other trails and paths veer off the route. Entering Balmacaan Wood now, there is a beautiful stretch through ancient trees with huge boughs.

Ignore a clear track left downhill and continue on the white marker opposite to loop around a duckpond. A steep descent after this leads you out onto a track near Balmacaan Farm. Follow this straight ahead to a junction and turn left, passing another information board at the entrance to these woods, and follow the track back to the giant redwood near the start of the walk.

■ Marker post on the red route in Craigmonie Woods

WALK 20

Explore the national nature reserve as you climb high on Britain's only waymarked mountain route

Start/finish Car park a few miles west of the Beinn Eighe Visitor Centre off the A832, near Kinlochewe
Distance 4 miles
Surface Rough, rocky and steep in parts but clearly waymarked path throughout
Map Mountain Trail booklet available from visitor centre; OS Explorer 433

■ The lone pine

Every step offers something spectacular on this magnificent walk up into the foothills of Beinn Eighe in Wester Ross.

It's a steep climb from the shore of Loch Maree to the so-called 'conservation cairn' but the views – particularly over the loch to Slioch, as well as of Beinn Eighe itself – are truly breathtaking.

Go through the underpass from the car park and stay on the left of the burn, not crossing the wooden bridge but instead following a mountain symbol into the woods on a marker post.

At first the route rises gradually through the ancient Caledonian forest but it leads to a waterfall on the Alltan Mhic Eoghainn, which you cross at a bridge before the way becomes rockier and steeper.

The mountain symbol seen near the start is repeated along the route, on rocks as well as posts, to reassure you that you are still on the right path.

You scramble through the rocks until the way eases to a gentle walk near the high point of this route at 550m above sea level. A cairn marks this point but, for me, the best view of the two Munros on Beinn Eighe comes from a little further along the path as it drops to a series of lochs.

This is a magnificent place to stop and enjoy the panorama of the high summits beyond the shimmering surface of the lochs.

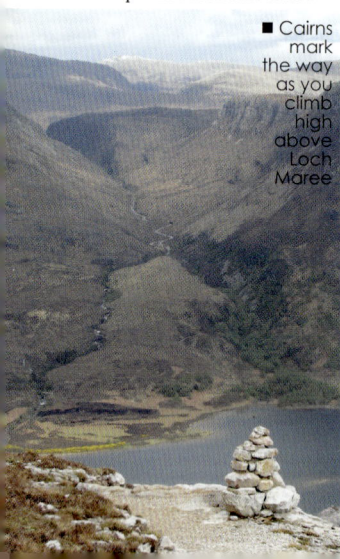
■ Cairns mark the way as you climb high above Loch Maree

Despite this being a route anyone can follow, this is still serious mountain territory at any time of year and I have seen the weather up here change from warm sunshine to snow and hail in midsummer, so it's essential to be prepared for any conditions.

The bare landscape is nowhere more apparent than at the appropriately named Lunar Loch, so called to commemorate the 1969 moon landing, but perhaps more relevant to the grey but beautiful surroundings.

From here, the route begins to drop and you can really appreciate the magnificent Slioch ahead.

Beyond the lone pine, marked with another cairn, there is a huge gorge plunging down ahead and the path has been fenced off to warn unsuspecting walkers of the danger.

Soon the route moves away from the edge and, as you re-enter the forest, you meet up with the shorter woodland trail. Take a left to join it and follow the markers through the trees back to the small wooden bridge near the underpass.

Map labels:

N

Loch Maree

A832

Woodland Trail

P

Rhu Noa

Lone Pine

Steep cliffs!

Allt na h-airdhe Gorge

To Kinlochewe

Lunar Loch

Mountain Trail

Cairn/viewpoint

Loch Allt an Daraich

■ Beinn Eighe over Loch Allt an Daraich

■ A delightful little bridge teeters over the edge of the river

A quiet walk beside a fast-flowing river that showcases some magnificent 19th century engineering

Start/finish Beauly railway station
Distance 5.5 miles
Surface Tarmac, earth and stone vehicle tracks, woodland path
Map OS Explorer 431

The odd thing about old bridges is that they look so much better from below than when you're using them for the purpose for which they were intended.

That magnificent view of the Lovat Bridge from the River Beauly is saved until last on this gentle stroll from Beauly. It's a flat walk with some lovely views of the surrounding hills, as well as a fairytale castle across the water.

From the railway station in the village, turn left to head away from Beauly towards the bridge on the pavement. On the corner, cross the main road carefully and follow the tarmac lane directly ahead.

The route sticks to this private road as it trickles all the way down to the river past trees and fields and then, suddenly, you see the red sandstone of Beaufort Castle sticking out above the already high trees. If you asked a child to draw a castle, this would be it. Once the house of the Frasers of Lovat, the castle, built in 1882, has round towers and turrets and is topped off with a Scottish flag flapping above.

Towards the end of the road,

Beauly riverside

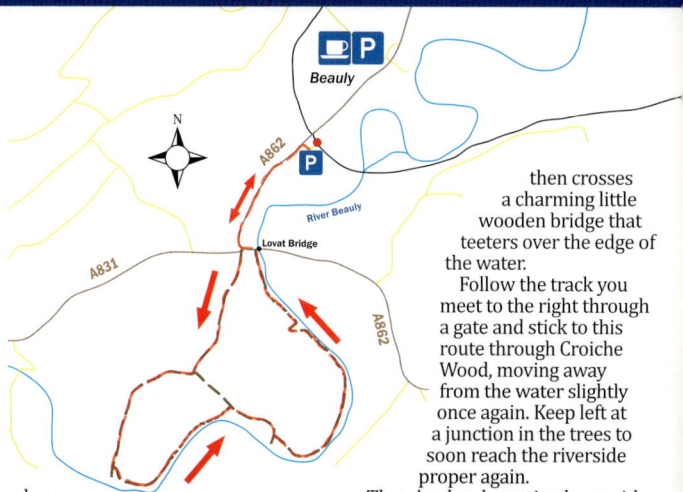

then crosses a charming little wooden bridge that teeters over the edge of the water.

Follow the track you meet to the right through a gate and stick to this route through Croiche Wood, moving away from the water slightly once again. Keep left at a junction in the trees to soon reach the riverside proper again.

There's a lovely section here with the water rushing alongside you as you meander along the wide track.

Soon you see that magnificent view of the Thomas Telford masterpiece, the Lovat Bridge, a grade A listed building built in 1810.

Pass through a gate and stick to the track behind some houses. Head to the stables ahead and keep right on the track nearest the river to emerge at the edge of the bridge.

Carefully cross the main road again and follow the pavement back up to Beauly.

where tracks lead off left, right and centre, take the one to the left to reach the water's edge and pass a small fishing hut.

Keep to the track as it moves slightly away from the water, which you can still hear, until you see a clearly defined path shoot off straight ahead on a bend in the track.

The track ends by the river but this delightful little path wriggles through deciduous woodland, cuts in front of an impressive white fishing lodge,

■ The A-listed Lovat Bridge near Beauly

WALK 22

Get close to Loch Ness on this easy stroll with spectacular views

Start/finish Dores Inn
Distance 3 miles
Surface Forestry tracks and woodland paths
Map OS Explorer 416; OS Landranger 26

Skirting the shores of the magnificent Loch Ness, this popular little walk gives incredible views down the Great Glen.

It takes you around Torr Point, which juts out into the heart of this legendary stretch of water, as it takes you on a gentle stroll through this delightful woodland.

There's parking at Dores beach, just behind the inn, off the B862 south of Inverness. Take the path that runs behind the Nessie hunter's caravan on the beach and go through the children's playground onto a track.

Just after the line of a fence, take the fork left to head around the point. The track stays within the trees around here but clearings between it and the shore open up the lovely views.

There is no problem finding the way as the track swings north-east and then your view is directed towards the north end of the loch where it is much narrower.

You can see steep drops down to the water on your

■ The track leads into woods behind the beach

■ An Torr in the trees from the popular destination of Dores beach

left at first, but soon the track drops and you find yourself on a level with it. There is even a spot you can plod out into the water where it is shallow – but be careful not to disturb Nessie!

Soon you will reach a gate at Aldourie Pier, with views across the small private marina to Lochend on the far side of the water. Go through the gate then, immediately after a concrete building, head right on a less well-worn track which goes straight uphill.

Turn right on the clear track at the top and follow it as it twists along the ridgeline of An Torr, ignoring what seems a clear path left at one point.

As the view looking south down Loch Ness comes back into view,

take the hairpin bend left in the track and keep following it, even when it becomes no more than an eroded line through the trees.

It brings you out, I assure you, at a fence overlooking fields across Strath Dores – home to the RockNess music festival in the summer. You can now see Dores across the strath and take the right turn to head back into the woods towards Loch Ness.

Take any of the eroded routes left to meet a track below, which will take you back to the fork in the track near the start of the walk.

From the fence, you can follow the path back to the start or head down to the beach and follow it along to the inn.

WALK 23

One of the most dramatic low-level walks in the Highlands

Start/finish Car park at head of Loch Affric
Distance 11 miles
Surface Vehicle tracks, paths with possible river crossings
Map Harvey British Mountain Map – Knoydart, Kintail & Glen Affric

Trek deep into the heart of wild Glen Affric on this truly spectacular circuit.

It's a popular route with walkers, and for very good reason. The going is mostly straightforward and involves very little climbing, yet you still find yourself immersed in a different world.

At the half-way point, you are in the middle of nowhere, well on the way to Kintail, on the west coast of the Scottish mainland, surrounded by a number of magnificent mountain ranges.

The Affric hills lie to the north, the Glen Shiel tops south and the Kintail ridges and Beinn Fhada are due west. What a place to find yourself in!

An excellent bridge at Athnamulloch is the key link in this memorable route, which begins at the end of the public road from Cannich to Glen Affric – a long, slow, twisting drive which may be impassable in winter conditions.

There's a large car park here, and the walk begins by going left out of its entrance down a track to a bridge. Cross it and go through a gate, climbing a short distance to meet another track which emerges from the south side of Loch Beinn a' Mheadhoin and turn right onto it.

This track leads you all the way along the south of Loch Affric and, as you progress, the views west get more and more dramatic. Once out of the woods, you cross the Allt Garbh and climb a short distance until Mam Sodhail and Carn Eighe come into view across the water.

Further along, the hills of the Cluanie horseshoe appear to your left and the Kintail summits can be seen ahead as you pass the end of the loch.

At a bend in the subsequent river, fork right

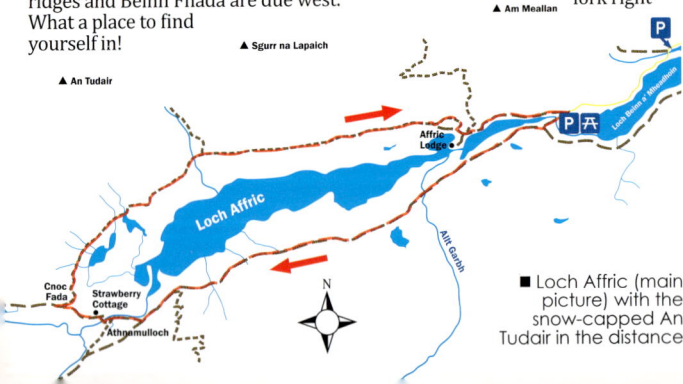

▲ Am Meallan

▲ Sgurr na Lapaich

▲ An Tudair

P

Affric Lodge

Allt Garbh

Loch Beinn a' Mheadhoin

Loch Affric

Cnoc Fada

Strawberry Cottage

Athnamulloch

N

■ Loch Affric (main picture) with the snow-capped An Tudair in the distance

onto another track towards a group of scattered buildings at Athnamulloch.

Cross the bridge to pass the beautiful Strawberry Cottage – a private hut owned by the An Teallach Climbing Club – and continue another 400m or so to a junction in the track.

The route ahead leads to the remote Alltbeithe youth hostel and beyond to Kintail, but this walk turns sharply right to head behind Loch Coulavie and around the northern side of Loch Affric.

There's a different atmosphere on this side of the loch as you leave the vehicle track behind and follow a clear but sometimes soggier path east. After wet weather there's a fair chance that the few river crossings will leave you with drenched feet, but I find the views over the delightful loch and the ancient Caledonian forest usually make up for any discomfort!

After passing through a fenced area where young Scots pine are protected to help regenerate the native forest, the path drops down to near Affric Lodge, where it diverts around the edge of some estate buildings to meet a tarmac vehicle track that leads back to the car park.

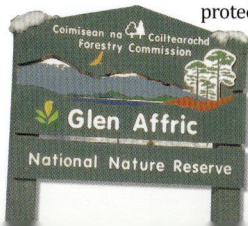

Coimisean na Coilltearachd
Forestry Commission

Glen Affric

National Nature Reserve

Discover a natural wonder hidden in the woods above a Ross-shire village

Start/finish Evanton
Distance 2.5 miles
Surface Woodland paths, quiet minor road
Map OS Explorer 432

Lying discreetly in the peaceful woods that rise up on the slopes behind the Ross-shire village of Evanton, the Black Rock Gorge will take you by surprise.

You can hear the trickle of water below as you approach, but nothing prepares you for that first glimpse of the huge chasm that is cut through the rock.

Nothing in the area shouts about this magnificent natural feature that is so close at hand.

There are a couple of walking signposts directing you towards the gorge but that's it.

Don't expect a fence to protect you at the edge of this massive drop, which dives straight down for over 100ft between dark, dank, slippery sandstone.

It's an eerie place up here, just a stroll from the centre of Evanton, where there is a small car park with bike racks off the B817 opposite the Cornerstone bookshop.

Turn right out of the car park and follow the pavement past the Novar Arms Hotel and across the Allt Graad. Turn left after the bridge up the Glen Glass road and keep left at a fork as the road rises.

■ You'll hear the water pounding through the Black Rock Gorge (left) before you can see it

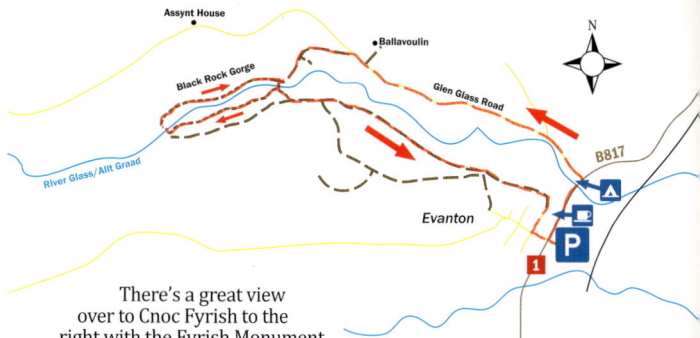

There's a great view over to Cnoc Fyrish to the right with the Fyrish Monument adorning its summit.

The monument, an imitation of the gates of Negapataum in India, was built in 1782 on the orders of Sir Hector Munro of Novar to provide work for the unemployed.

Look out for a green sign pointing left to Black Rock Gorge down a forestry track. Ignore a first path left after a clearing but follow a second path left which leads a very short distance to a bridge.

Still, there is no sign of the chasm but as you approach the bridge – there it is!

The woods seem so calm yet the water has scoured out the rock over centuries, leaving this great chasm in its wake.

Over the bridge, head upstream to the right to another bridge and cross the spectacular gorge again. Go right to head back to the other bridge, which you should

cross again but, this time, turn left on the far side to climb to a junction with a forest track.

Go left here and head down through these delightful woods, with the sound of the river far below still echoing in the trees.

At a turning point where four tracks meet, keep to the left one beside some fields and enjoy the lovely views down over the Cromarty Firth in the distance.

After passing some houses you end up on a residential street which you follow to a give way sign. Turn left here to return to the main road opposite the start point.

Ceum Path
Creag an Uillt Ghrànda
Black Rock Gorge   500m
Coille Bhaile Eòghainn
Evanton Woods

Get close to nature on this wonderful walk taking in the forests and roads around Carrbridge – ending with two spectacular bridges

Start/finish Carrbridge
Distance 10.5 miles
Surface Forest trails, tracks and paths, some very boggy; fords; tarmac cycle track; quiet road sections; busy road crossings
Map Trailmap, Strathspey Map 4; OS Explorer 403

Surrounding the delightful village of Carrbridge are woods that are perfect for walking and cycling, and this circular route offers plenty of variety.

■ Fording the Allt Lorgy on the old military road can be tricky at times

There are superb historic bridges as well as deep fords to cross, pine forests, birch trees, hidden paths through the woods, ancient ruins and military roads.

The walk starts at the main car park in the centre of the village, where there is a tourist information panel and picnic tables, as well as public toilets.

Turn left out of the car park and then left down the quiet Carr Road. Where the road bends right, turn right past Carr Cottages following a cycle route 7 sign and a wooden sign marked 'Woodland walks' and go through a gate into the forest.

Follow the main route through this lovely pine forest until you come to a sharp right turn in the track with a gate straight ahead. Go through the pedestrian gate onto open ground and cross a burn by means of a single plank before cutting diagonally right round the corner of a fence.

■ Sluggan Bridge now forms part of the National Cycle Network Route 7 between Inverness and Glasgow

It's boggy here so I'd advise following the higher ground to the right as you parallel the fence to meet a 4x4 track, which you join and head right, up into the woods.

This track continues up into a pretty birch wood before meeting a locked gate higher up, where you can easily hop over the fence and continue ahead on a clearer track.

At a clearing where you meet a parallel track, take a path to the right, passing under an electricity line and into the trees. You soon arrive at another gate, where two sections of tree trunk offer a superb stile, and drop down to Docharn farmhouse, where you meet the cycle route 7 again on a hairpin bend. Go left here and follow the access road all the way down to the A95 road.

You should use the separated cycle route when you reach the junction, which means you need to turn left, cross the main road, then turn right to cross the Boat of Garten road and follow the bike route signed towards Carrbridge and Tomatin.

After crossing the A95 again further on, the traffic-free part of the cycle route ends at the B9153.

Cross this and take the access road opposite for Kinveachy Lodge, which leads you under the railway line and across the busy A9 trunk road.

Continue towards the lodge on the private road until just before you reach the buildings, then turn right, almost back on yourself, on the highest of a ▶

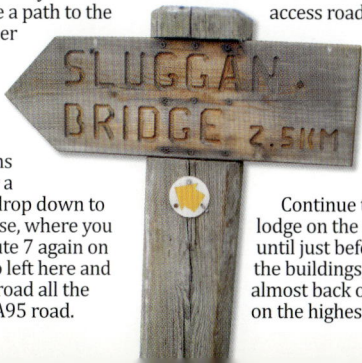

▶ number of tracks which lead in that direction. There are great views across to the Cairngorms from this point.

Where the track forks, keep left and continue over a crossroads. Soon, stay left on General Wade's Military Road towards Lethendryveole as a track meets you from the right.

Further on, after a cattle grid, stay straight ahead and go through a gate to the top of the hill, where there's yet another gate to pass through.

Now there's a long straight downhill until the track bends steeply left to the ford, which can be quite deep and fast-flowing at times.

If you don't want to just 'wade' through, you can usually find

■ Sluggan Bridge from the edge of the River Dulnain

somewhere to cross upstream to the left.

Continue along the track, going straight on at a crossroads, until a gate where you cross straight over the quiet road, hopping the low fence opposite to soon descend steeply and meet cycle route 7 once more.

Turn left and follow the track to Sluggan Bridge, which is believed

■ Carr Bridge (below)

to have been built as a replacement to the original in the 1830s. After crossing the wonderful arch bridge, turn right immediately behind a ruin and enter the trees by a gate.

Follow the boggy track and keep right where you meet a higher track. At a junction further ahead, turn left and cross a high stile then ford a stream and continue on the delightful path as it drops down to the riverside again.

When you reach a field, the now faint path cuts slightly away from the river to meet a more obvious route between two fences just before a clump of birch trees. Follow this to just before a gate to the house, then turn right to cross a pedestrian bridge and join the track beyond. At the end, you have to

cross the A9 again, then go through the red gate opposite and drop down under the railway.

After a short incline, keep an eye on your right for a new-looking gate which leads you down towards the Ellan Bridge. Go through the gate and follow the path round to the right to exit the field by a smaller gate beside the bridge.

Don't cross here but instead follow the riverside path as it meanders back to the village. On reaching the road in Carrbridge, turn right for a spectacular view of the packhorse bridge after which the village is named.

The car park is up the road on the left, but after that trek, you might want to test out one of the cafes or hotels before you take your boots off!

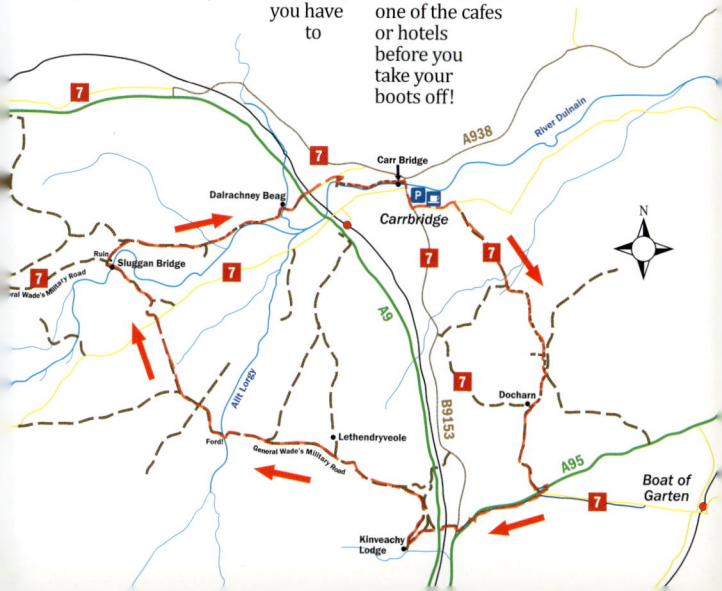

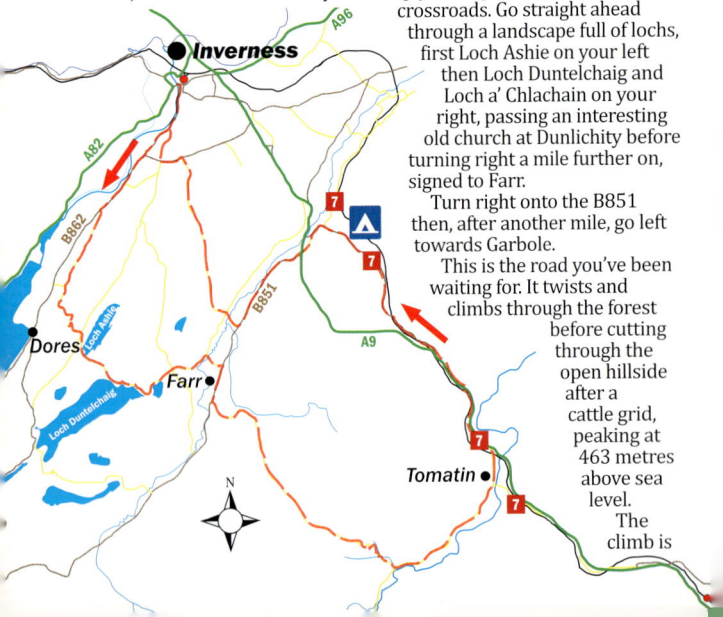

CYCLE 1

Spin past the wind farm over the northern edge of the Monadhliath mountains before a rolling descent into the city

Start/finish Whin Park, Inverness
Distance 48 miles
Surface B-roads, minor roads and traffic-free tarmac cycle path
Map OS Landranger 26, 27 & 35

The magnificent road that snakes its way over the Monadhliath mountain range is the highlight of this electric route.

It climbs past massive turbines, carrying you from Strathnairn into Strathdearn, with the chance to stop and visit a local distillery the other side of the hills.

From Whin Park, where there is plenty of parking available, head down river past the archive centre and cross the Ness Islands on your right. When you reach the far bank, carry the bike up a few steps and head right onto the B862.

This road heads all the way to Dores but I prefer to take the back route from Scaniport, about 3 miles down the road, to follow a single-track road with time to take in the glorious views to the Great Glen ahead.

At a give-way junction, head left and cross the burn before climbing steeply through the forest to a crossroads. Go straight ahead through a landscape full of lochs, first Loch Ashie on your left then Loch Duntelchaig and Loch a' Chlachain on your right, passing an interesting old church at Dunlichity before turning right a mile further on, signed to Farr.

Turn right onto the B851 then, after another mile, go left towards Garbole.

This is the road you've been waiting for. It twists and climbs through the forest before cutting through the open hillside after a cattle grid, peaking at 463 metres above sea level.

The climb is

■ Ben Wyvis from the high road which snakes over the Monadhliath

fairly long but not relentless by any means and you need to take care on the way down as the surface becomes loose on the narrow bends, as well as there being a couple of gates which can be closed across the road, so please leave these as you find them.

At the junction, turn left and follow the single-track road to the Findhorn Bridge then go left onto the road, part of the National Cycle Network, into Tomatin. Just past the village is the distillery.

Continue on the NCN Route 1, taking care where it crosses the A9 after a layby before joining the B9154 through Moy.

After a sharp little downhill, Route 1 is signed right to Inverness.

Ignore this and continue round the left-hand bend, forking left past a couple of houses on a track which

■ An underpass means cyclists can avoid crossing the busy A9

leads to a private underpass you can take to meet the B851 the other side of the A9.

Follow the road 2½ miles or so to Inverarnie, where you turn right past the shop, over the River Nairn and up the hill to a crossroads. Inverness is now signed 4 miles down the hill.

It's not long before you can just freewheel down the B861 and enjoy the spectacular views over the city and the Kessock Bridge to the Black Isle.

Shortly after reaching houses, you'll meet a big roundabout. Turn left onto a shared-use path along to the Essich roundabout, where a right turn down Stratherrick Road will lead you back down to the B862 near the Ness Islands. A right turn takes you the few yards to the steps from where you rejoin the outward route.

CYCLE 2

Experience cracking off-road cycling to be enjoyed in the forests around Strathpeffer

Start/finish Strathpeffer Square
Distance 17.5 miles
Surface Off-road vehicle tracks and singletrack, short minor road and A-road sections
Map Strathpeffer Trailmap, available from Square Wheels bike shop in the square

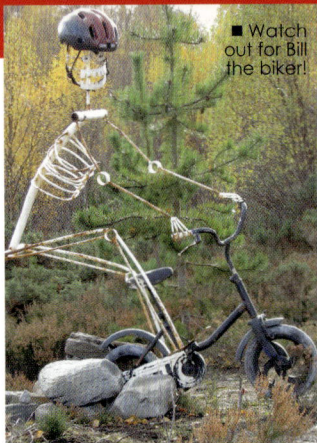

■ Watch out for Bill the biker!

The tracks and trails around Strathpeffer make it a place to visit on two wheels time and time again.

There are plenty of easy surfaces to enjoy in the surrounding area but this is the home of the 24-hour Strathpuffer mountain bike race, so you can also find plenty of exciting twisty singletrack.

Most of these trails have been built by the good folk at Square Wheels bike shop in the village, so that's the place for advice on riding the testing stuff.

This route allows the rider to take to the fireroads and take in the stunning views – with the chance to detour to Rogie Falls – but also gives a taster of some of the more testing singletrack, for those up for the challenge.

Turn right onto the main road from the bike shop and follow a sign further up the hill which reads 'Public Footpath to Garve 7' off to the right. Go left behind the Round House, following another sign to Garve past the beautiful Loch Kinellan.

After a short climb up from the loch, take a path left through the gorse just after a gate to join a better path beyond. It's soon a smooth downhill ride with the chance to do a few bunnyhops to avoid the drainage channels built into the path.

At a wooden sign, keep left towards Contin to meet the fireroad down the hill. Go right onto it to head towards Rogie.

A detour to Rogie Falls means taking a long track downhill which you'll have to come back up to continue the route. But it's worth it to see the lovely waterfalls and the fish ladder when the salmon are leaping.

Further along the fireroad, go through Rogie Farm then turn right towards Heights of Fodderty, going left soon after to pass under the railway and up to a crossroads.

Turn right here and follow the fireroad past Wyvis Plant and Power and up the hill, bearing right at a junction until a fork in the track. The left fork takes you high up into the foothills of Ben Wyvis, with fantastic views as you go.

From the top there is a speedy descent but watch out for the turn-off to Heights of Keppoch – you need to head straight on through two metal

Strathpeffer natural trails

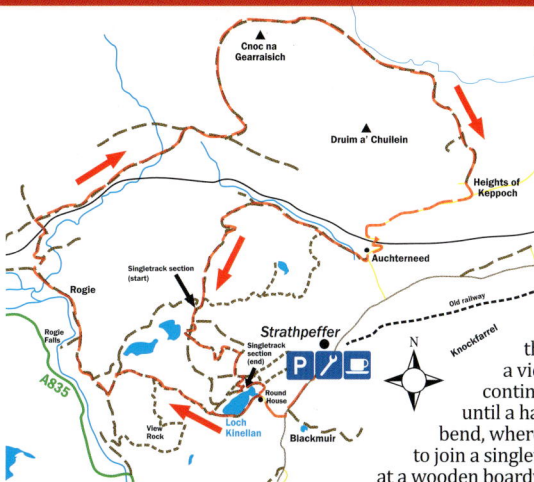

Go right onto a path here, signed off the road to Contin, and pass through the sawmill and a gate to join a track beyond, ignoring the footpath left to Contin en route. Stay with the fireroad to a viewpoint and continue downhill until a hairpin right bend, where you leave it to join a singletrack section at a wooden boardwalk.

Follow the twists and turns of the excellent singletrack until it dumps you out at a good track.

Turn right to go through a gate, then take the next left until a sharp right takes you back on yourself up to a bench. The track down to the right is an exciting steep descent which meets a track above Loch Kinellan. Turn left onto it, then right back to the Round House to rejoin the outward route.

posts at a 90-degree right bend. This track leads you bumpily downhill, passing through two gates and past a few houses before meeting the minor road at Heights of Keppoch.

I love the views over Knockfarrel and Dingwall from here and it's a good time to enjoy them while there is an easy section after turning right onto the road. Keep on the tarmac until a very steep descent just the other side of a level crossing.

Loch Kinellan

Travel deep into the country on this quiet road ride into the moors above Cawdor

Start/finish Cawdor Village Green
Distance 25 miles
Surface Minor roads
Map OS Landranger 27

There's plenty of history as well as fantastic wild views on this trip through the Nairnshire moors.

Much of the ride follows the old military road between Fort George at Ardersier and Ruthven Barracks, near Kingussie, which was built to help quash the Jacobite rebellion after the Battle of Culloden.

The route starts at the lovely village of Cawdor, where there is a small car park opposite the Village Green tea shop. Head right out of the car park and right at the road to head uphill past Cawdor Castle. This 14th century building is still home to the Cawdor family and is a popular visitor attraction with its impressive interior, gardens and wood.

Continue 2½km to a fork at Little Urchany where you turn left, soon joining the National Cycle Network Route 1 for a short distance before ignoring the cycle sign left as you drop down through the trees.

To visit the grave of an unknown clansman who was injured in the Battle of Culloden in 1746 and staggered to this point before dying, keep going over the Muckle Burn at a tarmac ford.

The grave, shown on the OS map, is marked by a stone on the right-hand side of the road just after a sharp left-hand bend.

Retrace your route back over the burn and take the dead-straight road left. The views are quite open here

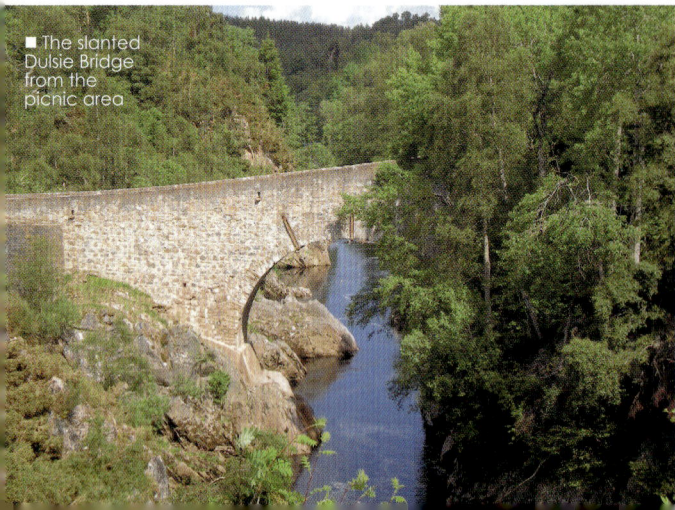

■ The slanted Dulsie Bridge from the picnic area

Cawdor

B9090

Little Urchany

Clansman's Grave

A939

N

Boath

Old Military Road

Dulsie Bridge

River Findhorn

Drynachan

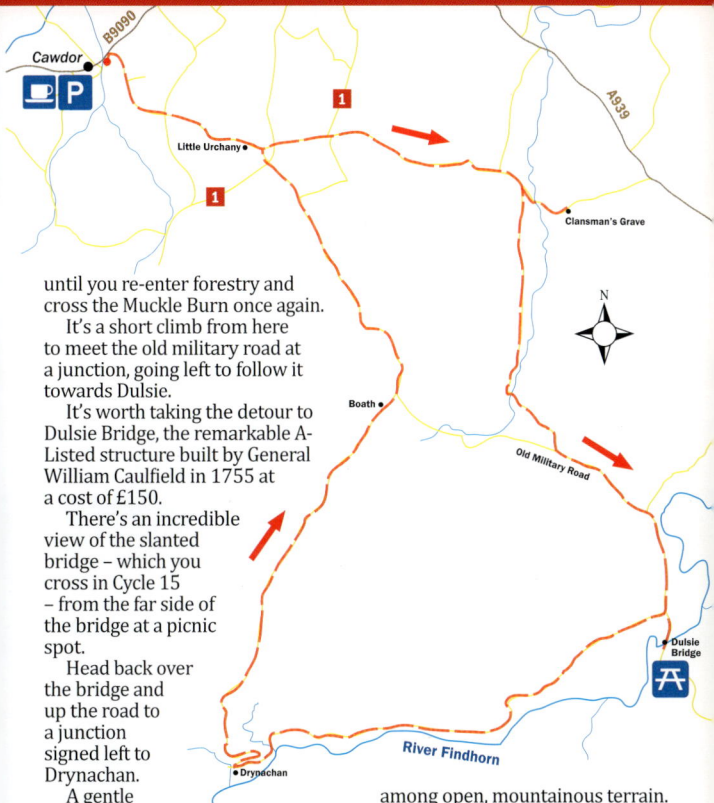

until you re-enter forestry and cross the Muckle Burn once again.

It's a short climb from here to meet the old military road at a junction, going left to follow it towards Dulsie.

It's worth taking the detour to Dulsie Bridge, the remarkable A-Listed structure built by General William Caulfield in 1755 at a cost of £150.

There's an incredible view of the slanted bridge – which you cross in Cycle 15 – from the far side of the bridge at a picnic spot.

Head back over the bridge and up the road to a junction signed left to Drynachan.

A gentle climb through the trees is worth it for the steep descent and open views of the River Findhorn you are rewarded with after Banchor. You're right at the end of the public road when you reach Drynachan. At the white building, turn right back on yourself to climb up through a beautiful bit of pine forest, emerging at the top among open, mountainous terrain.

Your eyes are easily distracted up here but the road is largely straight, meeting the old military road again at Boath then rolling down to meet the outward route at Little Urchany.

As you freewheel down the hill, enjoy the views over the Moray Firth then turn left at the bottom to reach the car park and tea shop.

CYCLE 4

Visit a friendly village at the end of a quiet Black Isle road

Start/finish North Kessock
Distance 14 miles
Surface Minor roads, short B-road section, tarmac cycle track
Map OS Landranger 26

Sitting at Kilmuir looking across the Moray Firth and listening to the waves gently lap against the shore is a wonderful experience.

The peaceful village lies at the end of a quiet road on the Black Isle peninsula and this route is a great way to get there.

It is possible to walk to Kilmuir from North Kessock but only at low tide, while the road down from Drumsmittal is always an option.

Starting from the large car park opposite the North Kessock hotel, head back up the road towards the A9 junction and turn right onto the shared-use path just before the roundabout. Turn left to cross the road and follow the cycle route through an underpass.

When you emerge at the top of the ramp on the far side, turn left, following the shared-use path until the painted give way marker. Carefully cross this high-speed slip road to the far side and follow the path right, joining the minor road up towards Drumsmittal.

Suddenly you are a world away from the busy road and onto a quiet country lane which climbs through the trees. Take the first road to your right, signposted to Kilmuir. It bends left past the car park for Ord Hill forest then

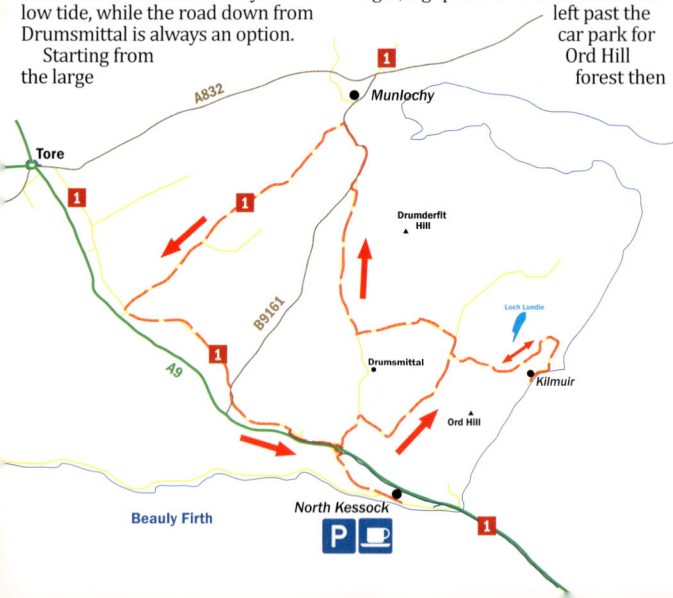

■ Looking across the bay at Kilmuir to Ord Hill

meanders along until a junction, where you turn right down the dead-end road to Kilmuir.

As you're whizzing down the hill, don't think about the climb back up – that will take care of itself later. For now, just appreciate the wonderful narrow lane and the incredible view out over the firth as you near the village.

Head right at the bottom and pause at a bench next to a red telephone box to enjoy the panorama from the coastline to the Kessock Bridge and Ord Hill towering above Kilmuir.

I like to gently pedal to the end of the friendly village and there are craft shops and other things to see along the way.

Now it's time to head back up the hill and turn right at the top then left towards Drumsmittal a short distance ahead. At an unsigned T-junction, turn right and pass the wildlife park before descending to the B9161.

Go right and follow the road over a narrow bridge then, just after entering the 30mph speed limit at Munlochy, turn left onto a minor road.

This is one of my favourite roads to cycle on as it is flat most of the way and usually quiet, apart from the odd tractor! It also passes the Black Isle Brewery at Allangrange before continuing to a junction where the cycle route to North Kessock is signposted left.

Follow this route, going right then left to cross the B9161 again and continuing on a minor road until you leave the road to the right near a layby and follow a cycle track back to the underpass.

CYCLE 5

Look out for Nessie on this challenging circular trip around the world famous loch

Start/finish Whin Park, Inverness
Distance 71 miles
Surface Half off-road on forest tracks and singletrack; half on mostly minor roads; very hilly throughout
Map Harvey Great Glen Way; OS Landranger 26 & 34

Capture your imagination with this epic route round Scotland's largest fresh water loch.

Loch Ness is a magical arena and cycling round its entire length gives you a great feeling for the area – and, you never know, you might just spot the monster!

The circuit of the loch is a superb outing, whether you do it in a day or stay overnight in Fort Augustus.

For this route, you follow the Great Glen Way on your way south, then return on excellent quiet roads on the far side of the loch. This avoids having to use the busy A82, which twists and turns and isn't a great place for cyclists to spend much time.

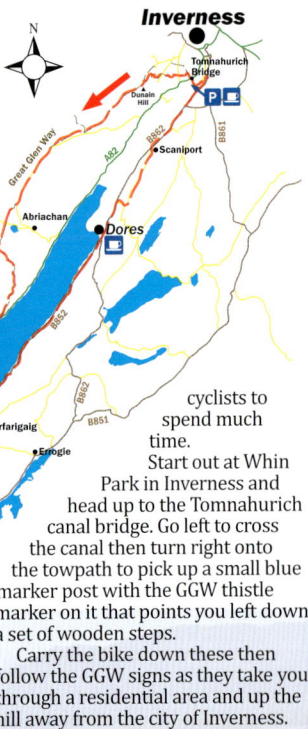

Start out at Whin Park in Inverness and head up to the Tomnahurich canal bridge. Go left to cross the canal then turn right onto the towpath to pick up a small blue marker post with the GGW thistle marker on it that points you left down a set of wooden steps.

Carry the bike down these then follow the GGW signs as they take you through a residential area and up the hill away from the city of Inverness. It's a tough climb but once you get behind Dunain Hill (see Walk 6) the gradient eases and you're away.

The GGW uses a mix of forest tracks, singletrack and roads as it makes its way through Drumnadrochit, out to Invermoriston and through the forest to Fort Augustus. The route is well signed but it's a long 38 miles to reach the far end of the loch as it twists and turns with some big climbs and descents, so allow plenty of time and go well prepared.

You'll be rewarded with occasional but spectacular views down the Great Glen.

There are plenty of cafes in Fort Augustus to refresh yourself before the big ride back to Inverness, which begins with another big climb up Glendoe.

Continue over the canal swing bridge and fork left onto a minor road as the main road bends right. It's around 5½ miles up the steep hill – with only a couple of sections of respite – to the roadside cairn marking the summit at the Suidhe viewpoint.

After all that effort, you do earn a speedy descent along to Whitebridge following General Wade's Military Road. This was his first route, completed in 1727 and linking Inverness with Fort Augustus

■ A view of Loch Ness along the off-road section near Invermoriston

via Essich and Whitebridge.

The shore road, which you turn left onto towards Foyers, was added in 1733.

Head through Foyers on the B852, which has a number of ups and downs – there is no real rest on this ride! Follow the road through Inverfarigaig (see Walk 2) and onto Dores (see Walk 22), with great views north as you hug the shore of Loch Ness.

Just over a mile after leaving Dores, turn right onto a minor road at the top of a hill then go left just before crossing a burn. Follow this road to Scaniport, where it emerges back at the main road and turn right back towards Inverness.

Cut left shortly after Drummond Crescent meets the B862 to cross the Ness Islands back to Whin Park.

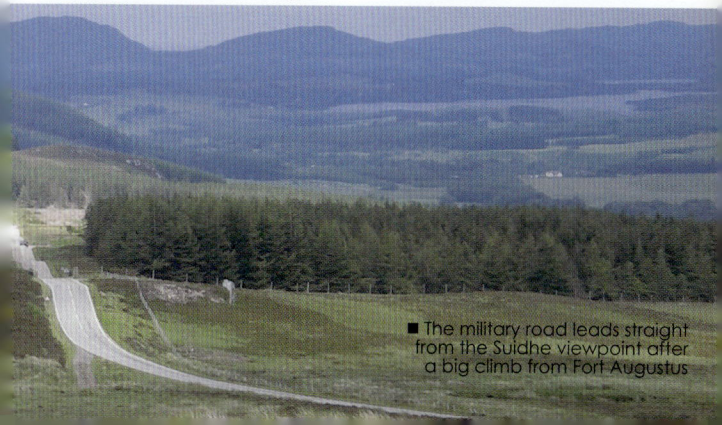

■ The military road leads straight from the Suidhe viewpoint after a big climb from Fort Augustus

CYCLE 6

Get splattered with dirt on this adrenaline-pumping route on the outskirts of Inverness

Start/finish Balloch Community Woodland, near Inverness
Distance 9.5 miles
Surface Muddy forest track followed by minor roads, B-road section and more forest tracks
Map OS Landranger 27

There's a twisting track hidden in a forest that provides a tremendous link from the National Cycle Network east of Inverness through to the village of Tornagrain.

It's muddy in parts – even on a dry day – and, combined with a couple of local roads, this circuit makes a fun little route when you want a blast of dirt!

While it's possible to use this track as a through-route from Inverness,

this shorter ride starts at a small parking area just beyond a railway bridge on the minor road down into Balloch from the B9006 turn-off near Culloden Battlefield (see Walk 14).

There's a green sign marked 'Balloch Community Woodland' pointing down the track, and this is the way to get going.

You soon pass the line of an old fence, bypassing an ageing stile, and continue on the main route. Turn left at the first main vehicle track and drop slightly for a few hundred metres, when you turn right on a bend.

The route to Tornagrain is fairly straightforward from here, as you keep on the clear track, watching out for any forestry work.

A clearing after crossing Red Burn at a bridge offers views out over the Moray Firth to Ben Wyvis but further on the soggy surface means keeping

■ The well-surfaced track emerges at the end of the Feabuie road

Tornagrain

A96

Cantraywood

Balloch

Feabuie

P

B9006

1 7

Culloden
Battlefield

B851

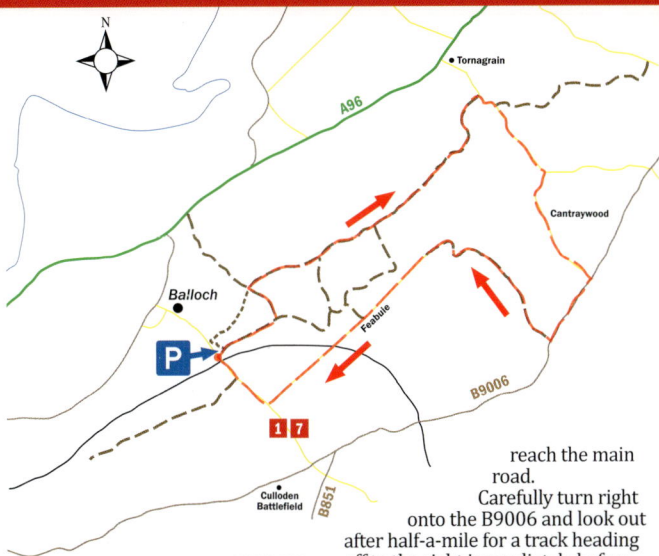

your eye on the track is just as important.

I guarantee you won't come back clean from this ride but the adrenaline is superb as you splash along the 3½ mile track to Tornagrain. The village itself lies a few hundred yards downhill to the left once you hit tarmac by a cottage, and it's worth dropping down here to see the open views across the firth.

Going back up the hill, as though you'd turned right when you emerged from the woods, follow the road up to an unmarked right turn and follow this lovely narrow road past a 'castle' until you reach the main road.

Carefully turn right onto the B9006 and look out after half-a-mile for a track heading off to the right immediately before the road curves left at an obvious bend.

Take this well-surfaced track uphill through a nice section of open forest, beautiful on a clear sunny day as it twists through S-bends and down to a gate at the end of a tarmac road.

Go along the dead straight road, which kinks over the burn and under the railway line, to a T-junction. Turn right, joining the National Cycle Network down towards Balloch.

Check you brakes now for a fantastic freewheel down the hill and under the railway to the parking area on your right.

■ Passing Loch an t-Seilich after Gaick Lodge

An off-road adventure over two high passes going into remote glens

Start/finish Ralia Cafe, near Newtonmore
Distance 50 miles
Surface Tarmac and earth cycle path, minor roads, short sections on main road, good vehicle tracks, 2-mile walking section on narrow mountain path, fords
Map OS Explorer 394 & 402

Exploring remote glens like the ones through the Gaick Pass is what makes mountain biking in the Highlands so much fun.

For me, there's no other way to get to some of these wonderful, remote places, and the tracks through the Gaick are great for cycling. One part in the middle requires walking for a couple of miles but it's no hardship for the fulfilment of one of the best routes in this part of Scotland.

You can start at the Ralia Cafe, just off the A9 near Newtonmore – or even at the railway station in the village. From Ralia, go left out of the car park and follow the cycle route onto the old A9. Cross one minor road then take the next one right towards Dalwhinnie, following National Cycle Network Route 7 all the way.

At a T-junction, go left to join the A889 and pass the distillery on the way through the village. Just before reaching the junction with the A9, turn right where the cycle path is clearly marked.

There's a warning sign here about the route, which climbs to 457 metres above sea level and has no food or shelter for 30km. In our case, it's more like 30 miles, as this route turns through the Gaick before getting back to civilisation the other side of Drumochter!

This fantastic route roughly follows the line of the A9 on a mixture of loose gravel cycle path and tarmac, reaching the summit of Drumochter with surprisingly little effort as the gradient is never severe.

Head down the other side, still on NCN Route 7, until you come out at a public road near Dalnacardoch Lodge. Turn left on the road, leaving the cycle route now, and very carefully cross the busy dual carriageway.

A sign on the far side points up the track: 'Public Footpath by Gaick Pass to Speyside'. Follow it up through the trees and past a communications mast onto the open hillside.

Continue along this fine vehicle track, passing a cairn and some ruins before dropping to cross the Edendon Water by a plank bridge. Not far along, it crosses back via a concrete bridge or ford – depending how wet it is!

Eventually the track reaches the ruins of Sronphadruig Lodge and fades to not very much. It actually turns left to ford the river (expect to get your feet wet on this route!). You should cross here then, 100 metres or so further up the track, look out for a narrow walkers' path on the far side of the burn. Find a safe place to cross – or use the dam further up the track if it's too dangerous – and follow the path above the beautiful Loch an Duin.

At the far end, the path crosses the inflow (which must be forded again) before rising to meet the end of a landrover track. It's mostly downhill from here and, other than a few potentially tricky fords to negotiate, fairly straightforward riding to Gaick Lodge, where the track improves.

There's a stone nearby to commemorate the deaths of five men killed in an avalanche here in January

1800. It just goes to show how hostile an environment this can be.

The route continues past Loch an t-Seilich to a dam, from where it is tarmac all the way down Glen Tromie to meet the B970.

Turn left to cross Tromie Bridge and pass Ruthven Barracks, now back on the NCN Route 7, which you follow left in Kingussie and back through Newtonmore to Rialia.

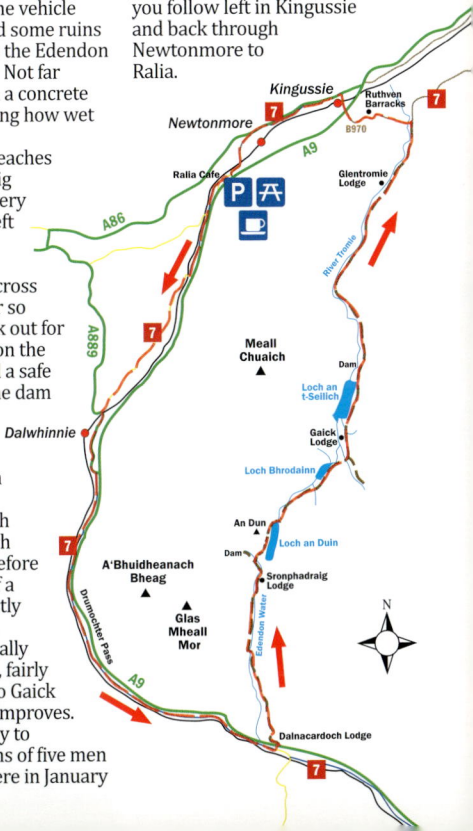

CYCLE 8

One monster hill from the shore
of Loch Ness is the focus for this
tough but exhilarating ride

Inverness

Start/finish Tomnahurich Bridge,
Inverness
Distance 20 miles
Surface Earth and stone
canal towpath, short section
on busy A82 before minor
roads, then good but
bumpy tracks
Map OS Landranger
26

Great Glen Way

River Ness

Caledonian Canal

• Blackfold

Dochgarroch

A82

Abriachan

Loch Ness

To Drumnadrochit

Take the
challenge
of the
Abriachan
road which
rises from
Loch Ness-
side to
more
than
300m
above
sea level
in just
2km.

As the hill
comes into
sight, it looks a
daunting prospect, but
the first section is one of the
steepest parts and it does get easier...
well, kind of.

At least, when it's over there are
some fantastic flat and downhill
sections to enjoy on the return route
and there are great views throughout.

The route starts at the
Tomnahurich Bridge and follows
the left-hand bank of the canal
down the towpath for 3½ miles to

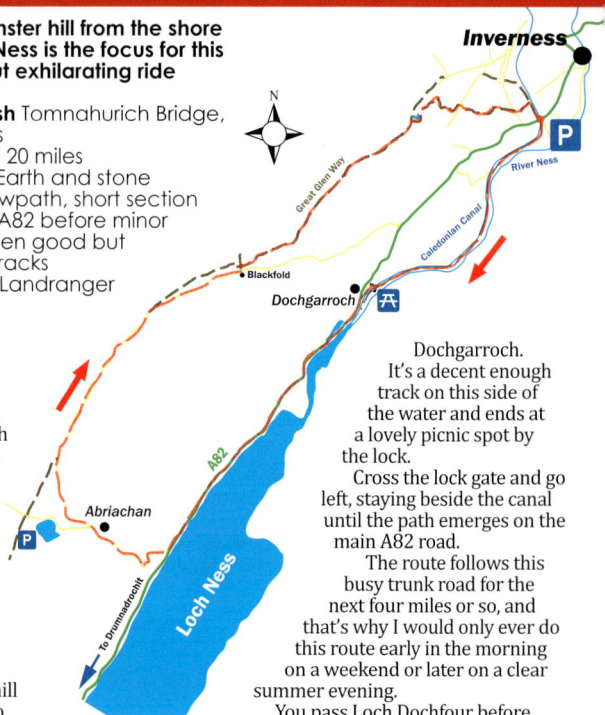

Dochgarroch.
It's a decent enough
track on this side of
the water and ends at
a lovely picnic spot by
the lock.

Cross the lock gate and go
left, staying beside the canal
until the path emerges on the
main A82 road.

The route follows this
busy trunk road for the
next four miles or so, and
that's why I would only ever do
this route early in the morning
on a weekend or later on a clear
summer evening.

You pass Loch Dochfour before
reaching Lochend and soon Loch
Ness itself comes into view. There are
plenty of parking spaces off to your

■ The hill winds its way up from the shores of Loch Ness

left so it's easy to get a break from the traffic or just take in the spectacular scenery.

Before you know it, there it is. The road to Abriachan is unmissable as it rises steeply away to the right ahead of you. Take care turning across this busy road (using the turning point on the left if necessary) and drop down the gears!

It's not long until you can look down on the distant sight of Loch Ness well below – and taking in the view certainly offers the perfect excuse for a rest part way up the climb.

After twisting round a few sharp bends, the gradient eventually eases before reaching a fork. Stay right towards Inverness, passing a field of Bronze Age hut circles about 1km on, which you can wander around if you choose. There is an information panel in an unmarked lay-by on the left, opposite the field.

Continue on the road past Ladycairn and speed on as far as Blackfold. These places are not signed so make sure you don't miss the turn off at Blackfold.

A track, marked with a Great Glen Way blue marker post, goes left opposite a farm about 100 yards before a forest plantation. Don't follow the first Great Glen Way marker you see after an S-bend, otherwise you'll end up on a path with an energy-sapping loose surface – take advantage of the good tarmac here to keep rolling along the quiet road until Blackfold. Take the track left, then turn right into the forest on the Great Glen Way after an information panel and bench.

You'll fare better on a mountain bike down here, although a hybrid would be fine if you take it easy.

Follow the blue markers through the forest on this old drove road then all the way down past a reservoir and new housing until finally reaching the canal at a few steps. Go right on the tarmac towpath to arrive back at the Tomnahurich Bridge.

CYCLE 9

Explore the beauty of the Black Isle peninsula on this road ride to Cromarty and back

Start/finish North Kessock
Distance 52 miles
Surface Mostly minor roads and quiet B-road with some tarmac cycle track
Map Sustrans Route 1, Aberdeen to John o'Groats; OS Landranger 26, 27 & 21

■ Resting at Cromarty

The charming village of Cromarty is a delightful place to visit, and what better way to get there than by bike?

The National Cycle Network can direct you all the way from Inverness, though this route starts over the Kessock Bridge in North Kessock, where there is a large car park opposite the hotel.

With all its quiet country roads, the Black Isle is wonderful for bike rides of any distance. This one, as its name suggests, is a tour of the peninsula and it takes in some incredible views of both the Moray and Cromarty firths, Fort George and Chanonry Point, the RSPB reserve at Udale Bay and the Cromarty Sutors (Walk 4).

Go left out of the car park to head back up to the road towards the junction off the A9. Just before the roundabout, go right onto the shared-use path and follow the NCN sign left across the road towards Munlochy and Tore.

The route goes through an underpass and follows the path on the far side of the dual carriageway until it heads left onto a minor road at a layby.

At a T-junction, go right then left past some kennels and, just over a mile up the road, turn right where the NCN Route 1 splits and follow the sign to Munlochy 2¾, passing the Black Isle Brewery a short way along.

Turn left at the end of this road to pass through Munlochy and go straight over at the stop junction to climb uphill towards Killen.

A couple of miles on, be careful not to miss a right turn at the end of a forested area to stay on the NCN. If you climb up to a TV mast here, you've missed it!

You should be on a straight road which continues for nearly five miles through Killen to a T-junction.

Turn right onto the B9160 then right onto the A832 which starts to descend quite steeply, but you'll need your brakes – and to drop down the gears – as you take a very sharp left turn back uphill on a minor road past Janefield towards Eathie.

This is a spectacular road which offers some of the best views I know of the Moray Firth back to Fort George and the famous dolphin-watching spot of Chanonry Point (Walk 18). It also passes the superb Learnie Red Rock mountain bike trails and another TV mast before dropping down to meet

SOUTH SUTOR VIEWPOINT

HARBOUR & LIGHTHOUSE
CROMARTY STUDY CENTRE
HISTORIC EAST CHURCH
GAELIC CHAPEL
HUGH MILLER'S COTTAGE

the A832 again, where you turn right into Cromarty.

Follow the NCN Route 1 signs down to the harbour and enjoy the wonderful views over to Nigg Hill and out to the Cromarty Sutors. You can also visit the National Trust for Scotland's Hugh Miller museum and some of the nice local craft shops in the village.

The return route follows the shore of the Cromarty Firth along the B9163, with outstanding views across to Easter Ross and Ben Wyvis.

Turn right at the T-junction after Jemimaville and soon veer right past an old cemetery towards the pretty Newhall Point.

Keep left at a small wooden sign to Balblair to climb back up to the B-road, where you turn right for a long steady ascent overlooking the firth.

Eventually, turn right towards Conon Bridge and drop down a nice twisty road that gives a great view of the

Cromarty Bridge. Carefully cross the A9 by the bridge and continue straight ahead on a nice single-track road until it turns sharply right, where you continue straight ahead on a minor road signposted to Ferintosh, then keep left at a give way sign to climb up to the B9169.

Go right and continue until you almost reach the A835. There is an excellent cycle path off to the left just before the junction, signed to Inverness and North Kessock.

Follow this to Tore, carefully over the busy roundabout (crossing the A9 again) and keep on the NCN Route 1 towards Inverness, turning right onto a minor road which meets your outward route at the NCN Route 1 split near Allangrange.

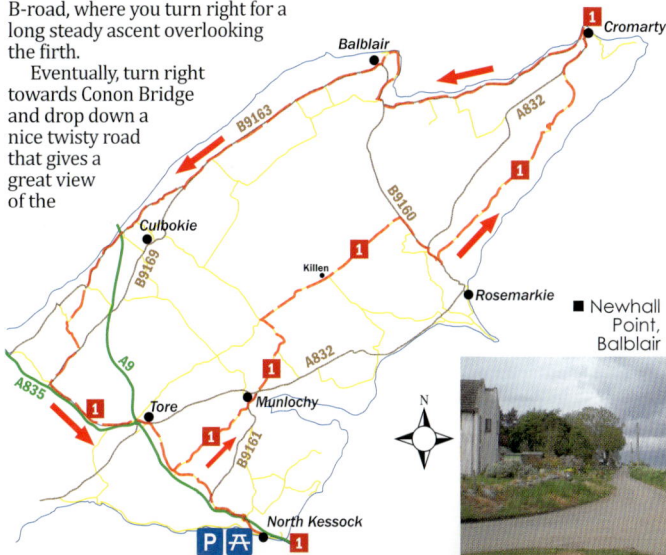

■ Newhall Point, Balblair

CYCLE 10

Discover south Loch Ness – and some rare birdlife – on this peaceful cycle tour

Start/finish Inverness High Street
Distance 29 miles
Surface Mostly minor roads, some B-road sections
Map OS Landranger 26

■ Loch Ness from the top of the hill above Dores

The ideal time to do this ride is in spring when there is a chance of spotting the rare Slavonian grebe at Loch Ruthven, but really it's a great cycle whatever the season.

The roads are quiet and the views extra special, from the panorama down Loch Ness from above Dores to the delights of Loch Ruthven then the view back into Inverness, where the route starts.

From the High Street, head down Bridge Street towards Ness Bridge and turn left before crossing the water. Bear right to stay beside the river then turn right at a T-junction.

At a large roundabout at Holm go straight ahead on the B862 Dores road.

I'd recommend turning left at Scaniport and following the beautifully quiet back road, simply because it saves a good few miles on the main road, as well as being less hilly. Turn right at a give way junction at Darris back to the main road then left down to the village of Dores,

with lovely views down the length of Loch Ness.

At the Dores Inn, take the left fork and prepare yourself for a hefty climb up the single-track road, which rises to 250 metres above sea level – with great views over Loch Ness and Meall Fuar-mhonaidh (see Walk 15) – and ignore a left turn signposted to Inverness at the top.

One mile further along, after a cattle grid, take a left turn signposted to the Loch Ruthven Nature Reserve. This drops to a beautiful narrow causeway across the head of Loch Duntelchaig.

The road beyond is just as spectacular and I reckon there's more wildlife to be seen along here than any other traffic.

In fact, as well as the hares and rabbits, you are more likely to come across sheep and cattle than cars on this spectacular piece of tarmac.

At the far end of Loch Ruthven, there is a small RSPB car park and it's a very short walk to the bird hide.

As well as the Slavonian grebes which nest here in the spring, there's also a chance of seeing ospreys fishing in

■ Loch Ruthven (right) attracts Slavonian grebes in the spring

the loch at this site of special scientific interest (SSSI).

Another mile brings you out at the B851. Turn left then left again towards Dunlichity a few miles on. You cross the River Nairn and follow this delightful narrow road to an old church at Dunlichity, built in 1758.

Go right then left up a steep hill to Bunachton then enjoy the ride across these rather exposed moors before descending to Essich after passing the electricity pylons.

The views down to Inverness and the Kessock Bridge from this road are truly magnificent – and all the better knowing it's an easy freewheel most of the way home now.

Turn right at Essich and the drop gets steeper still before emerging at new housing. Keep ahead at a roundabout and follow Stratherrick Road right down to Island Bank Road, where a right turn puts you back on your outward route.

■ Pedalling up the track through Glen Coiltie is worth the effort!

Follow a beautiful glen out of Drumnadrochit then pick up wonderful forest trails to visit an ancient monument

Start/finish Visitor Information Centre, Drumnadrochit
Distance 24 miles
Surface Mostly forest tracks, some bumpy ascents and loose descents – care required! Short sections on minor roads and main road to finish
Map OS Landranger 26

The well-preserved chambered cairn at Corrimony is around four thousand years old.

This 'passage grave' is of the same type as those at Clava Cairns (see Cycle 18) but this one is also worth a visit as you can still crawl through the narrow passageway to get to the tomb – if you are so inclined.

It is surrounded by a stone circle by the side of a very quiet road leading to an RSPB nature reserve at Corrimony, near Glen Affric.

It's possible to drive there, but you'll see so much more if you follow this cycle route from Drumnadrochit through the stunning surroundings of Glen Coiltie and Glen Urquhart.

Park at the Visitor Information Centre at Drumnadrochit, and the ride begins by turning right out of the car park. Take the second right onto Balmacaan Road just after the shop and takeaway.

Follow the road dead straight until you see a wooden signpost, directing you right to 'Corrimony 20km'. This marks the beginning of a long and bumpy climb up Glen Coiltie, but if you take your time and enjoy the remarkable surroundings, the effort is all worthwhile.

Go through the gate and follow the clear track as it winds its way upwards, with the sound of rushing water far below and some steep drops to the side to prove it.

At a massive turning circle, follow a small blue arrow up to the right – I'd advise walking this bit, if you haven't already resorted to that by this point!

Soon you get a fantastic view over Urquhart Bay and Drumnadrochit, then the gradient finally starts to relent and you can enjoy a long downhill section as you turn into Glen Urquhart, passing a link to Craigmonie forest walks (Walk 19).

Eventually you pass Balnain Bike Park – a practice area for expert mountain bikers only – then go sharp left after a gate to climb steeply up and round a corner to a communications mast.

Take the track to the right beyond the mast, now on the red route, and continue 2km or so to a track junction. Turn left to go uphill slightly, then go straight ahead rather than following the red route markers at this point.

This quiet little track offers incredible views to the Glen Affric mountains as it skirts through beautiful purple heather to cross the tumbling Allt Seanabhaile by a bridge. Climb up to a track junction – unmarked on the OS map – where you turn right for a long, fast descent to Shenval. The surface is loose and the gradient steep here, so take extra care.

Ignore a couple of tracks shooting off to your left and keep heading downhill until you reach a gate at a parking area. Go through it and follow the yellow route left to Corrimony at a wooden sign – using the other forest track, not the tarmac.

After a rare flat-ish section, look out for the right turn down to a gate, where a left turn onto the road takes you 1km to the Corrimony Cairn. There are no facilities or refreshments available here, so you'll need to come prepared, especially with all those climbs!

Once you've had a look around, head back along the same route as far as Shenval, and here follow the road past a few houses signposted towards 'Balnain 4.5km'.

Go through a gate and over the Allt Seanabhaile again, heading through farmland to another gate where you re-enter the forest. There's another stiff climb here but, once you've reached the top and turned left, the route is pleasantly undulating back to Balnain, where you go through a gate to enter a parking area.

Unless you fancy the big climb back up to Glen Coiltie, keep straight ahead and turn right onto the A831 for an easy 4 miles back to Drumnadrochit.

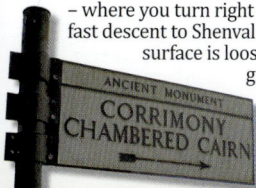

CYCLE 12

Have a blast as you leave the Highland capital behind on General Wade's route towards Edinburgh

Start/finish High Street, Inverness
Distance 15 miles
Surface Minor roads, forest tracks, tarmac cycle track, very short section on busy dual carriageway which must be crossed
Map OS Landranger 26 & 27

There's a wonderful little off-road track through Daviot Wood that provides a superb link to minor roads south of Inverness.

As a bonus, there's also a magnificent view back over the city from the track.

Unlike General Wade's route to Edinburgh, however, this one soon turns back to Inverness on a great road that says 'welcome to the Highlands' with spectacular views over the Kessock Bridge and Beauly Firth.

The route starts at the end of Inverness High Street, facing the river. Turn left past McDonald's on the corner and head up Castle Street, going through the traffic lights and turning left onto the one-way Old Edinburgh Road.

You now follow General Wade's route south out of the city. At the traffic lights, keep in the right-hand lane to go straight ahead before turning right 100 yards further on.

At a mini roundabout, keep straight ahead and continue to a large roundabout, where you can join a cycle lane to cross the road at a toucan crossing.

Follow the sign for Druid Glen off the roundabout and quickly turn right up a dead-end road signed Old Edinburgh Road South. This is a great, quiet road bordered with lovely trees and fruit bushes that climbs away from the city.

When you get higher up, take a look over your shoulder to get a first glimpse back over the city, a magnificent sight – but there is even better still to come.

Keep on going until the tarmac turns into a rough footpath, then follow a pedestrian sign left

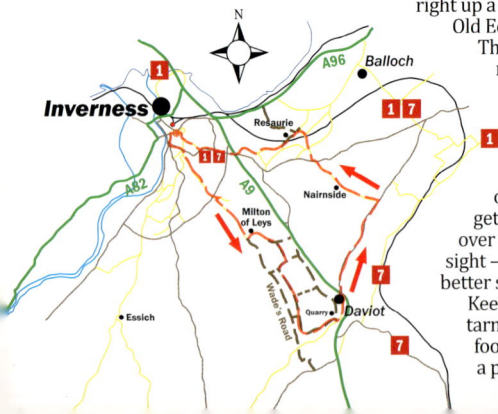

to Milton of Leys. Stay on the path to emerge near the end of Redwood Crescent, where you turn right onto Redwood Avenue. Go uphill gradually and continue until you reach Castleton Village.

Turn right here to join a track into Daviot Woods and look out for a wooden sign right to Daviot viewpoint at the first track junction. Take this track to climb up to the unmarked viewpoint, where it's worth a stop to look back again before entering the main plantation.

Enter the woods proper on an excellent little path and go right to follow the yellow route on good vehicle tracks. There's another uphill section before – finally – a big descent on a loose surface down to a quarry.

Go left onto the road, then follow a sign past the village of Daviot to Inverness (A9). Pass the beautiful old church at Daviot – once known to drovers as the 'kirk of the golden cockerel' due to its distinctive weather vane – to meet the dual carriageway.

Carefully turn left then cross the A9 to turn right towards Croy on the B851. Shortly after Forest Cottage, turn left at the first public road junction and climb again up to the hamlet of Nairnside. Once you emerge from the trees the views over the Moray Firth and Inverness are unbelievable.

For me, this is the best way to arrive in the capital of the Highlands.

Freewheel down to a T-junction where you go left then immediately right onto Tower Brae South. At the bottom, cross the road beside a bus stop and continue down Tower Brae North to join a road beyond a gate.

On a corner, turn left down a dead-end road through Resaurie to join the National Cycle Network Routes 1 and 7 towards Inverness.

You now follow the bike signs back over the A9 on a cycle track which meets Old Perth Road the other side of a busy roundabout.

Keep ahead at traffic lights past Raigmore Hospital and again at a roundabout before turning right at the next set of lights onto Kingsmills Road.

Continue at another set of lights then, at a speed hump, go left to follow the cycle route down a steep hill onto the High Street.

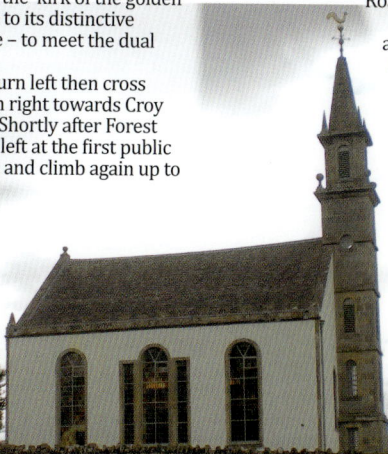

■ Daviot Church

CYCLE 13

A favourite ride for locals and a nice circular route for traffic confident cyclists

Start/finish Muirtown canal bridge, Inverness
Distance 25 miles
Surface Busy A and B-road sections, minor roads, traffic-free cycle path
Map OS Landranger 26

This great little route offers impressive views from every angle of the Beauly Firth and includes the popular focal point of Redcastle, complete with traditional red phone box.

The hardest bit of the predominantly flat circuit of the firth is deciding which way to tackle it.

Going clockwise, as described here, means getting the busier section of road out of the way first and enjoying the quiet northern shore of the firth on your return; though in truth it is a pleasure either way.

From the canal bridge, where there is a parking area beside a shop, head west through a series of traffic lights and follow the road through the village of Clachnaharry, which was built to house workers on the canal in the 19th century.

After crossing the railway bridge at another set of lights, it's onto the open road with a fantastic view ahead towards Beauly. Take care along here as it's a fast road and can be busy at peak times, though it is still a popular route for cyclists.

Pass through Bunchrew and, after around six or seven miles from the start point, you reach Inchmore. Opposite the Old North Inn at the far end of the village, fork left onto a shared-use path which follows the line of the road for a way until moving left to join a minor road.

Keep ahead here and cross a weak bridge, closed to motorised traffic. Turn left then follow the road right past Moniack Winery and through Cabrich on a wonderful country road that winds through this beautiful area on the edge of The Aird.

Eventually, the road emerges back at the A862 Beauly road, which you join to drop downhill under some power lines to the Lovat Bridge (see Walk 21). Follow the road sharp right to pass through Beauly and up a rare hill the other side towards Muir of Ord.

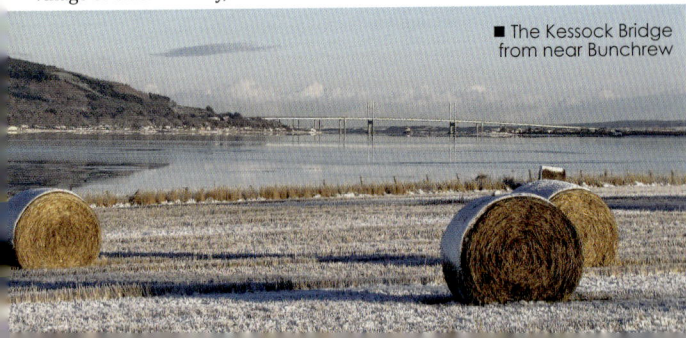

■ The Kessock Bridge from near Bunchrew

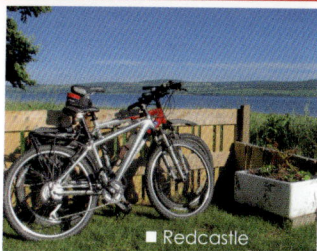

■ Redcastle

Before reaching the village, turn right onto the B9169 towards Fortrose and Cromarty, soon passing the Black Isle Show Ground.

Turn right to join the A832 towards Tore and, half a mile after dropping down through some speedy S-bends, look out for a cycle sign pointing right to Inverness down a minor road.

You now have miles of easy riding on glorious single-track roads, as you glide past a church at Kinellan and turn right to meet the shore at Redcastle, where the locals have provided a couple of picnic tables and a beautiful garden area for visitors to enjoy. It's a peaceful place to stop and take in the views.

The road hugs the shore all the way along as you pass a caravan site and the Kessock Bridge comes into view before reaching the village of Charlestown. Turn right at the T-junction to go through North Kessock and left up Old Craigton Road, where a cycle route leads up to the bridge.

There's a traffic-free path over the bridge and a right turn, signed to Inverness, at the bottom of a long freewheel, so test out those brakes! Follow the cycle path to meet the road, where you turn right then left to follow the shore past the harbour on National Cycle Network Route 1.

Follow the route right onto Portland Place just before the Shore Street roundabout, then turn right (leaving the cycle route) at a give-way to cross the Black Bridge.

Go left immediately the other side of the river, and follow the road along as it swings sharply to the right up Abban Street before swinging right then left onto Carse Road.

Turn left at the mini roundabout to pass the Co-op, then go right at a bigger roundabout to return to the Muirtown bridge.

■ Glen Affric mountains from above the Allt Garbh

An epic mountain bike adventure into the wild heart of Scotland's most beautiful glen

Start/finish Cannich Village Hall
Distance 29 miles
Surface Forest tracks, singletrack, some pushing/carrying required, steep climbs and descents
Map OS Explorer 415

Pedalling deep into Glen Affric, this challenging ride is not one for the faint hearted.

It involves more than 1000m of ascent, much of it on some rough, bumpy and boggy off-road trails.

You'll be dragging and pushing your bike at some points and you'll be a long way from civilisation, so you'll need to set off prepared.

Despite all that, it's a fantastic route. The views – as well as the sense of adventure – make it all worthwhile.

The village hall car park is on the left shortly after crossing the River Glass as you approach Cannich on the A831 from Drumnadrochit. To start, head back along this road and turn right towards Tomich immediately after the bridge. Follow the single-track road through the village then keep left at a fork, signed towards Plodda Falls (see Walk 5).

Continue past the falls car park, beyond Garve Bridge to Cougie. Keep to the road which twists right towards the pony trekking centre and take the second of two tracks, signposted to the Allt Garbh.

It's a decent wide track that rises gently and soon stunning views to Carn Eighe and the other north Glen Affric mountains emerge in the distance.

Stay right at an unmarked fork onto an older looking track. The going gets rougher down here and a series of short, steep climbs make it tough going.

Go through a large gate and drop down to cross the Allt

an Laghair either by a ford or a very rickety bridge – not advised for riding over.

A few more climbs take you to the highest point of the route, after which you need to watch out for a Scottish Rights of Way Society sign directing you right on a boggy path to Loch Affric.

After reaching the remains of an old fence, I'd recommend walking down the steep, narrow path and pushing or carrying the bike. The path stays east of the delightful Allt Garbh – rather than crossing it as the OS map suggests.

There are some nice spots to stop for a break by the water here before the path emerges at an excellent vehicle track above Loch

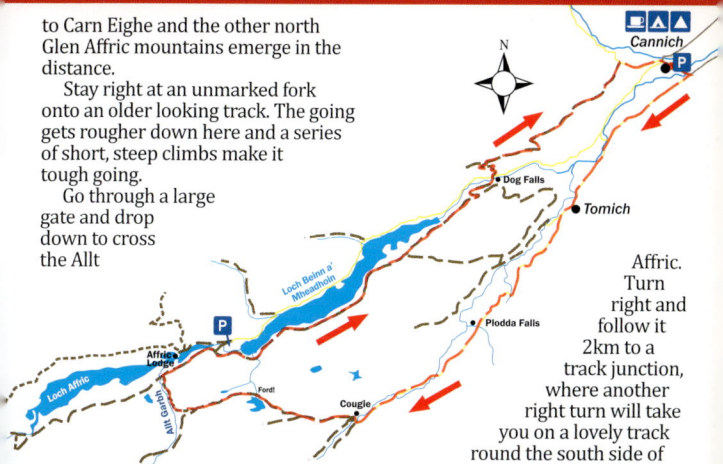

Affric. Turn right and follow it 2km to a track junction, where another right turn will take you on a lovely track round the south side of Loch Beinn a' Mheadhoin.

It's largely flat until near the end of the loch, where there's a steep climb followed by a fast descent which requires care. Take a left turn during the descent – watching out for walkers – to stay on the white waymarkers down to the Dog Falls car park.

Cross the road and go through a gate opposite, leading you onto an off-road climb which ends with a beautiful section of singletrack riding that dumps you out on a wide forestry track.

Turn right and follow it 4 miles or so to a gate to emerge on the Glen Cannich road. Go right and enjoy the freewheel down to the village. At the give way junction, go straight ahead to return to the village hall.

Public Footpath to the Allt Garbh

Scottish Rights of Way Society

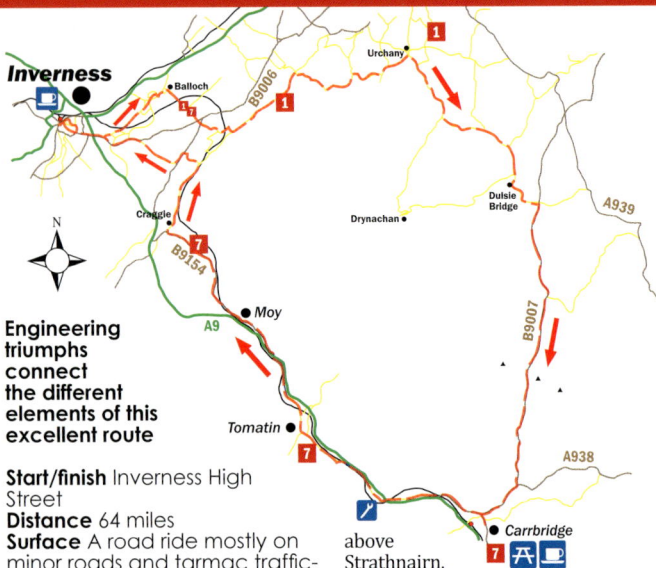

**Engineering
triumphs
connect
the different
elements of this
excellent route**

Start/finish Inverness High
Street
Distance 64 miles
Surface A road ride mostly on
minor roads and tarmac traffic-
free cycle path, with some
main road sections.
Map OS Landranger 26, 27, 35,
36 (or a good road map!)

Gorgeous country roads and
expansive views await the
determined cyclist willing to tackle
this challenging ride.

Its three notable crossings are
not the only highlights but Dulsie
Bridge, Carr Bridge and the Findhorn
Bridge at Tomatin are each full
of history.

Nearer the start of the
ride you also get to cycle
under the impressive and
imposing Culloden Viaduct
which carries the railway
600 yards on a curve

above
Strathnairn.

The route
follows the National Cycle Network
Route 1/7 from Inverness through
Culloden and Balloch to Clava Cairns.

Where the two route numbers
split at Clava Cairns, keep straight on
towards Nairn to pass under the 19th
century viaduct and steeply up to a
T-junction, where you turn left.

Keep on the cycle route as it
follows amazing single-track roads
with open views across the Moray
Firth to the Black Isle and Ben
Wyvis before passing through
forests.

Leave Route 1 near Urchany,
where a road sign points
right to 'Dulsie 6½' on the
old military road. Continue
over the slanted bridge to

a crossroads where you turn right towards Carrbridge on this high and exposed B road.

Assuming the snow gates are open, you'll get up to 384 metres above sea level – and enjoy dramatic views of the Cairngorm mountains ahead – before dropping down to meet the A938 for the last couple of miles into the village.

To see Carr Bridge itself, go left at the junction. You can't miss the remains of the old bridge, which was built in 1717 to reach the burial ground across the River Dulnain at Duthil (see Walk 25).

The journey back to Inverness begins on NCN Route 7, which means going back to the A938 from the village and continuing up the hill, left from the junction.

Just before the road turns to meet the A9, carefully take a right turn on a very quiet road which heads towards Slochd. Like much of the cycle route here, it uses the old A9, which skirts over the railway and under the new A9 before passing Slochd Hostel (cycle hire/repairs). Again, just before returning to the main road, the cycle route is signed left through a gate, following the old A9 up to Slochd Summit, squeezed between the railway line and the new road.

Joining another minor road, you then drop down to cross the Findhorn Bridge, a 1920s concrete structure which crosses the River Findhorn before the road flattens towards Tomatin. Beyond the village, a cycle track takes you along then across the A9 before joining the B9154 through Moy.

Turn right at the bottom of a speedy descent, signed 'Inverness 11' on the bike route, but take the first

■ Cycling under the Culloden Viaduct

public road left, immediately after a house and just before the railway bridge, at grid reference NH749428. Turn left after the steep climb up from the river crossing then right about 600 metres along the B851 at Nairnside.

There are spectacular views of Inverness and the Moray and Beauly firths as you drop to meet the B9006 at Westhill and turn left to rejoin your outward route at the junction with Caulfield Road North after a couple of miles.

The NCN route takes a slightly different return route into the High Street, going right onto Kingsmills Road at traffic lights to drop steeply down Stephen's Brae for an easy finish to this spectacular ride.

■ Spectacular view from
the road to Newtonhill

**A delightful circular road ride
between Inverness and Beauly
with magnificent views north**

Start/finish Old North Inn,
Inchmore
Distance 9.5 miles
Surface Quiet single-track
roads, B-road, short busy A-
road section; some steep hills
Map OS Landranger 26

Lying just west of the Highland
capital, The Aird is an attractive
rural area made up of croft land and
forestry.

Its steep slopes face north, giving
open views across the Beauly Firth to
the dominant summit of Ben Wyvis.

Most of this nice circuit is on minor
roads with little traffic and there is
plenty to see along the way, from the
Wardlaw Mausoleum at Kirkhill to
the winery at Moniack.

It starts at the Old North Inn on the
A862 Beauly Road, where there is a
large car park open to walkers and
cyclists as well as the inn's clientele.

Out of the car park, go right on
the B9164 to Kirkhill, crossing the
Moniack Burn before climbing
gradually to the village. The
Mausoleum, which dates from 1634
and was the burial place of the Lovat
Frasers, is signposted off to the right
from the centre of the village. It was
renovated in 1998 after falling into
disrepair.

Continuing through the village
on the main road, fork right after

The Aird cycle route

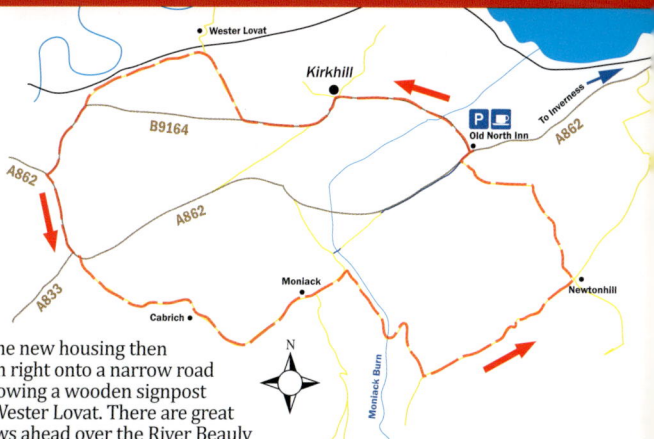

some new housing then turn right onto a narrow road following a wooden signpost to Wester Lovat. There are great views ahead over the River Beauly to the hills beyond.

Don't cross the railway bridge but instead turn left before it and parallel the railway line to Ferrybrae. Keep right to rejoin the B9164 and follow it downhill to the A862.

This is the busiest section as you turn left onto the Inverness road but you are only on it for about half a mile, when you carefully leave this road to go right towards Cabrich on a tight left-hand bend.

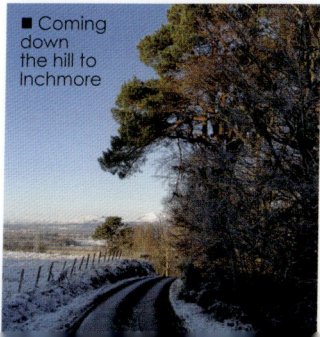

■ Coming down the hill to Inchmore

From here, the route follows excellent narrow minor roads all the way. It undulates through the crofting hamlet of Cabrich before curving left past Moniack Castle and its associated winery, which is open to visitors. The castle dates from 1580 and the Frasers have lived there ever since.

On a left-hand bend, turn right following a wooden signpost to Reelig Glen (see Walk 7) and follow the road as it enters the forest and twists over the Moniack Burn once more.

Get set for a steep climb round a hairpin bend and turn left near the top onto a road towards Newtonhill. The gradient soon eases but the spectacular views to your left from along this dramatic road will continue to take your breath away.

Turn left and check your brakes at the junction in Newtonhill for the exhilarating 2-mile descent back to the main road at Inchmore. The lovely inn is a short distance to the right.

CYCLE 17

An epic coast-to-coast traverse for well-prepared mountain bikers with lots of stamina

Start/finish Ullapool/Alness
Distance 50 miles
Surface Estate roads, rocky vehicle tracks, intermittent walkers' path, remote, steep in places, navigation skills required
Map OS Landranger 19, 20 & 21

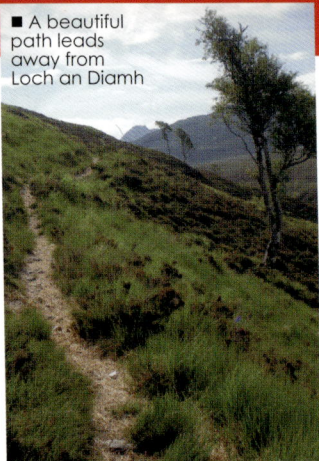

■ A beautiful path leads away from Loch an Diamh

This is a classic cross-country route that takes you from the west coast to the east through the beautiful county of Ross-shire.

It's a serious undertaking which uses mainly rough hill tracks, perfect for mountain bikes, with a little bit of tarmac at either end and a boggy, narrow walking section in the middle.

This fantastic adventure is a long day outing even for the fittest riders.

You are immersed in the mountains all day, with possibly the most remote Munro, Seana Bhraigh, an enchanting sight as you make your way between Glen Achall and Strath Mulzie.

The ride can start anywhere in Ullapool but, as this is a coast to coast route, I reckon it should start right by the sea, whether that's at the pier or on the shore-side campsite.

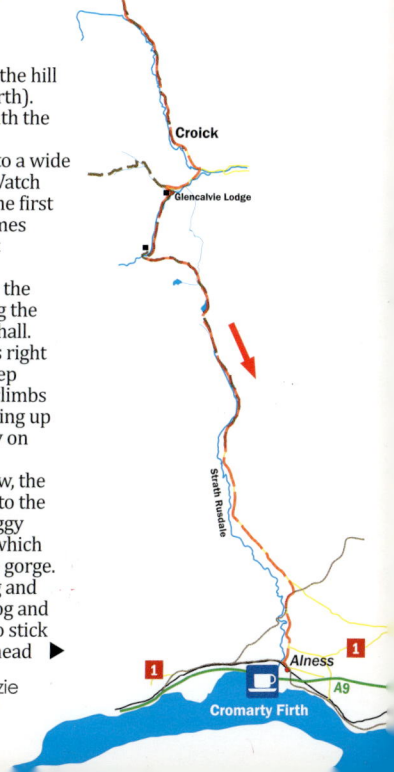

■ Loch Achall
near Ullapool

From the pier, head straight up the hill and follow signs for the A835 (North). You should meet the main road with the Ullapool River on your left.

Cross straight over the road onto a wide track, marked Morefield Quarry. Watch out for quarry traffic up here for the first mile or two before the track becomes tarmac and turns into an excellent estate road.

Cross a plank bridge and follow the road, which becomes a track, along the north side of the peaceful Loch Achall.

Where a pedestrian bridge goes right over to East Rhidorroch Lodge, keep left as the track gets rougher and climbs steeply – there's no shame in walking up here as the going gets pretty tricky on the loose stones.

With Loch an Diamh now in view, the track splits. Turn right to descend to the head of the loch and follow the boggy bay round to find a walkers' path which follows Allt nan Caorach above the gorge.

This is a 2-mile stretch dragging and carrying the bike uphill through bog and heather on a path that's not easy to stick to, but it's worth it for the views ahead ▶

■ Meeting the track in Strath Mulzie (left) with Seana Bhraigh beyond

▶ to Seana Bhraigh as you rise higher.

Finally you meet the track through Strath Mulzie at a red marker arrow and can enjoy getting back on the bike again. Go left onto the track and keep left again a mile ahead, down by the river.

Pass Corriemulzie Lodge and continue to Duag Bridge, where the obvious track goes right to cross the Abhainn Dubhag and past a shelter on the left. Another ½km on, fork right onto an older-looking track that climbs steeply.

It levels before reaching a track junction where you turn right and, higher up, fork left to parallel the fence to a kissing gate higher still.

A very rough track now bumps you down through a forest into Strath Cuileannach and you follow the river all the way to Croick, where a visit to the historic church is very interesting.

THROUGH ROAD TO ULLAPOOL
(30 miles)
no vehicle access

It is still possible to see where crofters who were kicked off the land during the infamous Highland Clearances of the 19th century scratched their names in the window of the church as they took shelter there to hide from officials.

A mile after Croick, turn right opposite a red phone box past Amat Lodge. Just before the tarmac road ends in a couple more miles, look out on your left for a sign for Glencalvie Lodge. Follow the track down left through the grounds of the lodge. Despite the 'Private, lodge only' signs, this route is a right of way to the glen beyond, so don't be put off.

Keep right of the river after passing through the grounds until you are out in the open again, where a plank bridge takes you over the Water of Glencalvie.

The track climbs gradually then more steeply as it swings round to the left and up to the highest point on the route at 437m above sea level. Continue to a nice little loch and, beyond it, follow a dead straight fence down the hill.

At the end of the fence, the track narrows to

■ Metal marker pointing back to Ullapool from Strath Mulzie

■ It's worth paying a visit to Croick Church at the half-way point

a path and then you hit a stone 'road block' which you'll need to carry the bike over, then there's a gate leading into a forest.

You now follow this track into Strath Rusdale and out to the public road at Braeantra. Keep straight ahead on the tarmac until you reach a main road at a T-junction some miles on. Turn right, then take the first left, signposted 'By-way to Alness and Invergordon'.

This road is a lovely downhill ride with views out over the Cromarty Firth on the east coast and you emerge on the buzzing High Street in Alness, where you might be glad of some refreshments!

If you're getting the train from here, the station is a few hundred metres along the road to the left.

■ The dead straight track beyond the little loch

Fort George

Moray Firth

Carse Wood

Nairn

Wester Delnies

Cemetery

B9092

Ardersier

Howford

B9101

Inverness Airport

A496

B9039

Loch Flemington

B9090

River Nairn

B9090

B9091

Cawdor

Croy

B9006

1

1

1

7

Clava Cairns

7

From ancient burial chambers to the home of the Black Watch on some tantalising country roads

Start/finish Clava Cairns, Culloden, Inverness
Distance 32.5 miles
Surface B roads and minor roads, main road crossings
Map OS Landranger 27

East of Inverness lie some fantastic country roads stretching out across Nairnshire, and this super route links up some historic attractions along the way.

Not only does it begin at the 4000-year-old Clava Cairns near the site of the Battle of Culloden, but it goes on to visit the Barracks at Fort George – built in the late 18th century in a bid to quash the Jacobite threat in the Highlands after that momentous event – and passes close by the 14th century Cawdor Castle.

There is a small parking area at the Cairns, which are signposted from the B9006 heading out of Inverness.

The ride starts by turning left out of the car park then left on the National Cycle Network towards Inverness and Culloden. Follow it up the hill to a give way sign at some cottages, where you turn right then right again to join the B9006 towards Croy. This is a fantastic undulating stretch and you'll soon find yourself at Croy, where you fork left signed for Ardersier. Drop down the hill on a superb single-track road past the Mains of Croy to a junction.

■ Clava Cairns

Clava Cairns & Fort George

Cross the main road here and go straight ahead past Loch Flemington, a beautiful spot I discovered purely by chance when cycling these quiet roads. There's a lovely view out over the loch, teeming with wildlife.

The road edges left past the houses to meet the A96. Cross this trunk road carefully to continue past Gollanfield and keep going until another give way sign. Here, go left to continue pretty much straight ahead then, after a sharp left-hand bend, turn right immediately after a house.

This road also bends left before, in the middle of a long straight, you turn right again where a very small sign points to the cemetery.

Turn left just after the wall at the far end of the burial site and go left again at the bottom to pass the shooting range, going right at the main road to visit Fort George.

Return the way you came but, instead of turning right up to the cemetery, keep straight on then go left at the next crossroads to enter Carse Wood. If you want to skip the visit to Fort George, just keep straight ahead at the cemetery and again at these crossroads.

This quiet road curves through the trees and climbs a short, steep hill to emerge at the B9092, which you turn left to join. In about a mile,

go right after the first house you see on that side of the road. A tarmac track leads you to the A96, which you must cross again and go straight over, passing the caravan site and heading over the railway line.

After some houses, go right then left to follow a minor road through Little Kildrummie to Howford, where you turn right to cross the bridge over the River Nairn. Immediately the other side, go left and follow the road up to a junction, where a right turn leads you uphill then back down to meet a B road.

Turn right onto it and continue straight on through Brackla then Cawdor, where there is a shop and pub, as well as the castle to visit.

Beyond Cawdor, fork left onto a minor road to continue straight on where the main road turns sharply right. This road meets the National Cycle Network again at Galcantray and continues until a cycle sign directs you right, down under the Culloden Viaduct to meet your outward route near the Clava Cairns.

■ The beautiful shore-side road at Redcastle en route to Muir of Ord

Set off over the Kessock Bridge for a road ride around Ross-shire

Start/finish Inverness High Street
Distance 40 miles
Surface Minor roads, some busy main roads, sections of tarmac cycle path
Map OS Landranger 26

This fantastic get-up-and-go route takes you out of the city in no time and all on good tarmac.

Starting in the centre of Inverness, you follow Bank Street up the River Ness from the bridge, then follow the National Cycle Network Route 1 under the Friar's Bridge and down Shore Street.

Once round the edge of this industrial estate, a magnificent view of the Kessock Bridge appears ahead.

Turn right just before going under it, then left at the cycle lane to join the bridge. Over the other side, turn left at some bollards to drop steeply into North Kessock and go right along the shore past the old pier.

A left turn beyond the village centre is signed to Muir of Ord – for cyclists at least.

This wonderful road to Redcastle hugs the shore all the way, then goes inland before you need to turn left through Milton past a beautiful old church to reach the A832. Turn left onto the main road here, going uphill through the S-bends before continuing straight on into Muir of Ord.

At a give way junction, take the road straight ahead to cross the railway then almost immediately go left, following the Ullapool road. You'll soon see and smell the distillery ahead – take a left just before it to pass the visitor centre and head gently up to Aultgowrie on a wonderful back road.

Follow this quiet route until it drops you down in the village of Marybank at a crossroads, where you go straight on to cross the Moy Bridge and turn left onto the busy A835.

This is the main trunk road west, so take care over the next two-thirds of a mile before turning right up a minor road signposted to Kinnahaird. After passing through the farm, this road rises to meet the A834 and a right turn will take you through Jamestown and through some twisting tarmac into the spa village of Strathpeffer.

Continue on the main road all the way to Dingwall 6 miles or so ahead. When you reach the traffic lights, go straight ahead onto the partly-pedestrianised High Street and follow it round past the railway station to another set of lights, where you turn left.

Soon you can pick up a good tarmac cycle track alongside the A862, which you

■ Sustrans milepost outside Dingwall railway station

can stay on as you swing left at the roundabout before Maryburgh.

At the next junction, the bike route uses a minor road past Leanaig before going right then left over a fantastic stretch to Tore. Carefully cross the busy roads at the Tore roundabout following Route 1 signs to Inverness and North Kessock, taking a right a few hundred yards after the roundabout to go past Redfield and the turn off to Cromarty.

Go right then left after a give way to pass Croftnacreich before leaving the minor road at a sign and following a tarmac cycle path alongside the A9. Go through the underpass and turn left the other side towards Inverness.

This soon puts you back on the bridge where you can enjoy the magnificent view back towards the city knowing you're almost there.

■ Looking down the zigzags into the Corrie Yairack itself

Follow in the footsteps of General Wade on a high climb over this famous mountain route

Start/finish Newtonmore/Fort Augustus
Distance 34 miles (plus 32 miles return to Inverness)
Surface Rough, eroded military road; single-track roads; sections on A roads; navigation skills required.
Map OS Landranger 34 & 35

The ascent of the Corrieyairack Pass is now a classic mountain biking or walking challenge.

The 'road', built by General Wade's men in one summer in 1731, links Speyside to the Great Glen and climbs to over 2,500ft above sea level.

That means you need to be prepared for a full Scottish mountain adventure, as there are no escape routes from this dramatic pass.

The remaining original stretch of Wade's road, between Melgarve and Fort Augustus, is the longest surviving example of its kind at around 12 miles long.

It's not possible to cycle every last bit of it – but the bits you can ride make up for the pushing and carrying you'll have to endure on the loose, rocky surface!

For this route, take the train to Newtonmore and follow the road out of the station to the main road, where you turn left to pass the shinty ground and a caravan site. Turn right just before meeting the A9 and follow the cycle route past Ralia Cafe and onto the old part of the A9.

At a sign for a holiday park, turn right onto the first minor road, signed to Laggan. At a memorial cairn in the first few miles, you get a view of the route ahead.

Turn right onto the A886 at a

T-junction beside a phone box, then turn right towards the village when you meet the A86. After about half a mile, turn left past a shop and follow the minor road past a glorious loch beyond the Spey Dam.

You cross one of Wade's classic bridges at Garva Bridge then go through the gate at its far side to climb up past plantation forests, still on tarmac. The road ends just before Melgarve, where the off-road challenge begins.

It's worth exploring in the woods by the Allt Feith a Mhoraire for the East Bridge, marked on the OS map. The bridge was repaired in 1984 by the Association for the Protection of Rural Scotland.

Go under or around a chain with a "Private" sign to join the first part of the original military road, which passes a bothy near the remains of one of the old bridges.

It's almost impossible to cycle any part of the long straight road now but eventually you can get back in the saddle for a while as you get higher up into the desolate Corrie Yairack.

The track curves to the left before climbing steeply up a series of magnificent zigzags, which are also difficult to ride up. Once at the top, a vast view opens up before you.

The ride down to Fort Augustus is on a better surface but still requires some serious concentration, as it is pretty bumpy. Take extra care on a weak bridge over the Allt Coire Uchdachan and on a very steep descent to a plank bridge over the Allt Lagan a Bhainne before heading down Glen Tarff.

There are spectacular views up Loch Ness as you near Fort Augustus before a series of S-bends down through Culachy Estate. Keep right at the bottom by a pond and soon reach a road block.

Go straight on onto a grassy path beside a burn which leads through a gate, then turn right onto the minor road, having finally conquered the whole pass. To reach the village, stay on this road to its end, then turn left. Fort Augustus is one mile ahead.

If you're planning on cycling back to Inverness, you can turn right at the give way sign and follow the second half of Cycle 5 up South Loch Ness.

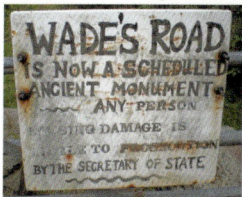

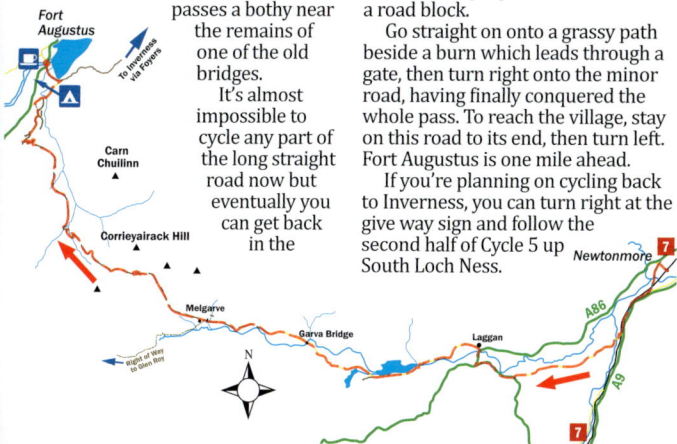

■ The stunning campsite at Durness in the far north-west

A beautiful two-day tour to the north-west corner of the Highlands

Start/finish Lairg
Distance 118 miles (Day one – 56m; Day two – 62m)
Surface Mostly single-track roads
Map OS Landranger 9, 15 & 16 or OS Road 1

Taking you to the north-west corner of the British road network, this spectacular excursion through the Highlands is road cycling at its best.

It takes you past shimmering lochs, through magnificent glens and under towering mountains, with an overnight stop on the cliffs of the spectacular north coast.

By starting at Lairg – just over an hour's drive from Inverness and also on the railway route north – this trip can be done in two days, making it perfect for a weekend adventure.

There's a free car park just off the main A839 Rogart road in Lairg, where there are also public toilets. From the car park, turn right to roll down the hill to a junction and then turn right towards Durness.

In a couple of miles, the route splits, with both ways signed to Durness! Take the left turn onto the A838 as it follows the north shore of Loch Shin, with Ben Hee visible ahead much of the way and Ben More Assynt across the water.

There's very little in the way of shelter among this seemingly wild landscape, but you do pass a hotel at Overscaig that serves drinks and food during the summer months.

Beyond here, the winding road passes a series of smaller lochs, popular with anglers, to reach Laxford Bridge – a rare junction on this fantastically enjoyable outing.

Turn right to cross the bridge, which was built in the 1830s, and soon climb a hill on a rare section of single carriageway road. At the turn-off for Kinlochbervie lies the Rhiconich Hotel, which is open all year and is the last place for shelter and refreshment before Durness.

With Foinaven and Arkle on its doorstep, this is a beautiful area for mountain lovers and there are amazing views as you pedal onwards on the single-track road. A long, speedy descent along this section helps eat up the miles but you may find yourself simply wanting to stop and breathe in the magnificent surroundings.

The sandy Kyle of Durness is passed, along with the junction to Cape Wrath at the north-west tip of the country, before rolling into Durness for an overnight stop. The busy little village has a campsite, youth hostel, hotels and B&Bs galore.

The first 20 miles of day two bring a fair number of hills as you skirt round the peaceful Loch Eriboll. Start by forking left in Durness to take a steep short-cut to Smoo Cave, then follow the A838 again as it hugs the impressive coastline.

The first junction comes after crossing the outflow from Loch Hope then climb up the first part of a longer 15% climb. Turn right, signed to Altnaharra, onto a wonderful narrow road with views ahead down Loch Hope with Ben Hope rising like a monument from its eastern shore.

A well-preserved Broch – an Iron Age defensive building – by the side of the road makes an interesting stopping point a few miles past a parking

area for the walk up the most northerly Munro.

Climb away from this point before a nice long descent to Altnaharra, the crossroads of the Highlands. Turn right and pass the village's hotel, another rare opportunity for refreshments, before following the National Cycle Network Route 1 up Strath Vagastie on the A836.

The high point is reached just before the remote Crask Inn, which is open all year, then it's a fine ride through Strath Tirry to meet the junction with the A838 two miles north of Lairg.

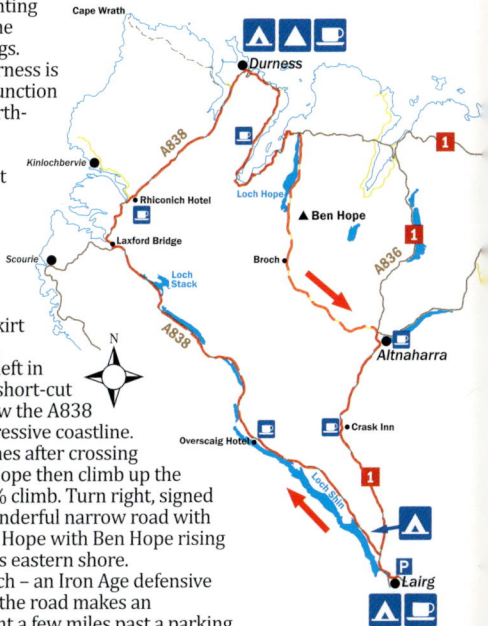

Follow the King's route across the Cromarty Firth on this Pictish discovery trail

Start/finish Inverness/Tain
Distance 40 miles one-way
Surface National Cycle Network on minor roads and tarmac traffic-free cycle paths. Seasonal ferry crossing (May to October).
Map Sustrans NCN Route 1, Aberdeen to John o'Groats

This right royal route offers that special treat of travelling in the Highlands and islands by bicycle – a trip on a ferry.

Only this one is just a stone's throw from the Highland capital, a perfect excuse to get some sea air and give the legs a good rest at the half-way point.

You leave Inverness by the National Cycle Network Route 1, crossing the Kessock Bridge and following the route across the Black Isle to Cromarty as described in Cycle 9.

That's a magnificent ride in itself, but catching the seasonal Cromarty Ferry means you can follow in the footsteps of King James IV of Scotland, who used this same route on his many pilgrimages to the shrine of St Duthac in Tain in the late 15th and early 16th centuries.

The view between the Cromarty Sutors (see Walk 4) is superb from the little ferry and – don't worry – the track you see heading steeply up Nigg Hill isn't your route ahead.

Leaving the ferry slip, head

The Cromarty Ferry operates between Cromarty and Nigg from May to October every 30 minutes during the day. For full details and prices visit www.cromarty-ferry.co.uk or call 01381 610 269.

NCN Route 1 to Tain

■ The ride begins with a crossing of the Kessock Bridge to the Black Isle

along the road past the old oil terminal and fabrication yard, then turn right onto a minor road towards the village of Nigg itself.

Here you pass Nigg Old Church, home to an impressive eighth century Pictish cross-slab stone, a highlight of the Pictish trail which passes here.

Continue to a junction, where you turn right towards the Seaboard towns of Balintore and Hilton of Cadboll, with fantastic views out over the Moray Firth. At Hilton, there are the remains of an old church and a replica of another Pictish cross-slab stone – the original now resides in the Museum of Scotland in Edinburgh.

The undulating route now turns inland, crossing the B9165 at a crossroads before passing close by the pretty Loch Eye, all the while following quiet minor roads with little more than farm traffic on them usually.

Go straight over another

crossroads then fork left at a junction to join the road between Portmahomack and Tain.

This road leads you right into the heart of Tain over the River Tain then the railway to a give way junction in the centre of town.

Straight ahead is the visitor centre and museum, with the route to St Duthac's Church down to the right before them. The impressive church was built between 1370 and 1460 to house the shrine to the saint, who was born in Tain and was once a popular figure.

To return to Inverness, the railway station is down the road beside the museum – or, if you're feeling up to it, you could return by the 'winter route'.

Follow cycle signs to Alness to cross the A9 and pick up the Scotsburn road if you fancy this option; otherwise, let the train take the strain and enjoy the views on your way back round the Cromarty and Beauly firths.

CROMARTY FERRY

The ferry runs between the end of May and the end of October subject to weather. To confirm ferry operation phone 07879 401659 or 07768 653674

CYCLE 23

Head down the beautiful Strathglass to the head of Glen Affric before a challenging return to the Highland capital

Start/finish Clachnaharry, Inverness
Distance 56 miles
Surface A roads and minor roads, optional short section on tarmac cycle track
Map OS Landranger 26

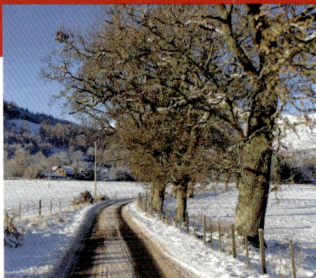

■ Link road to A831 at Struy

The ancient Caledonian forest, the wild mountain landscape, impressive lochs – Glen Affric is a wonder to those who venture there.

On this excellent road ride from Inverness, just getting there is a pleasure. It's a great way to get away from the city and catch a glimpse of this world-famous scenery.

Of course, a longer visit or plenty of return trips are worth taking to fully appreciate this magnificent area (See Walks 5, 10 & 23 and Cycle 14).

The gateway to Glen Affric, the village of Cannich, lies at the end of a triangle of roads which head outwards towards Drumnadrochit and Beauly. That's where you're headed on this outing.

From Clachnaharry, on the western edge of Inverness, take the A862 Beauly road as far as Inchmore, where you turn right into Kirkhill. Through the village, follow signs for Beauly and turn right once you meet the main road again.

Once over the rather narrow Lovat Bridge, where the road swings right to Beauly, go straight ahead towards 'Scenic Glen Affric'.

Climb a short way before taking the first public road left signed for Kiltarlity and drop down to cross the River Beauly on a single-track bridge with a view to a hydro power station upstream.

Up the hill, turn right towards Fanellan and Eskadale for a steep climb on a wonderfully narrow road. At a give way marker in Hughton, turn right to pass through Eskadale

■ River Glass and the quieter 'back road' up Strathglass

on the long and winding back road down Strathglass.

This road parallels the busier A831 the other side of the river, and there is a bridge at Struy which links the two. It's a long stretch with few obvious landmarks to indicate how far on you are, but the occasional open views you get ahead to Glen Affric are magnificent.

Eventually you hit the main road. A right turn here takes you down to Cannich, where there's a good cafe at the campsite, as well as a shop and a hotel.

Head out of the village the way you came, up the lengthy Kerrow brae before the road starts to undulate a little more. Keep on the main road for just over 10 miles from Cannich, passing the beautiful Loch Meiklie on your right near Balnain.

Your next turn takes you left, back towards Beauly, on the A833. The ominous sign at the bottom warns you what is to come – this is a 15% climb over three-quarters of a mile. What it doesn't tell you is that it gets steeper nearer the top.

Just when you think you must have the worst part of the

Culnakirk hill out of the way, it steepens and bends and saps your energy. Thankfully, that's the real climbing done with for the day.

The rest of the A833 undulates nicely through the lonely Glen Convinth, with spectacular views to the north and west, as well as closer to hand with The Aird to your right.

At the end of the road, go right for Inverness but turn immediately right again on the corner to Cabrich. This is a nice back-road section that lessens the time spent on the busy A862.

Keep straight on until shortly after the Moniack Winery, where you go left then right over a weak bridge that's closed to traffic. Follow the road beyond and keep straight ahead through a gate to use a nice little cycle path (ignore the gate and turn right at the give way to stay on the road) to Inchmore, where you rejoin the main road back to Inverness, seven miles beyond.

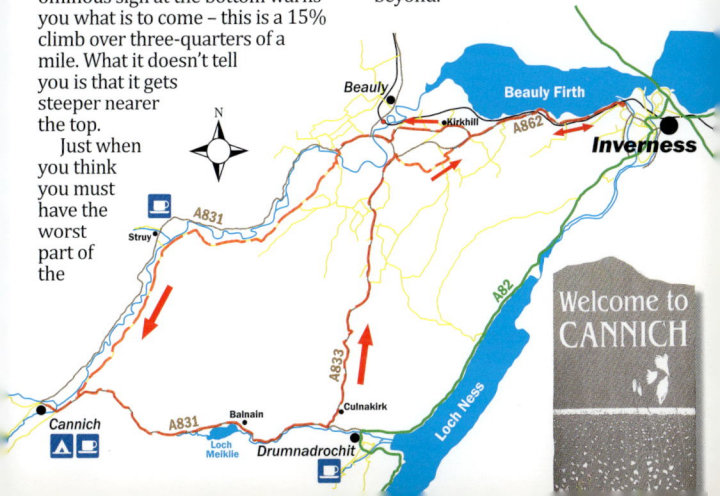

Moray Firth

Nairn

Brodie Castle

A96

Auldearn

Newmill

Ring Cairn

Whitemire

Enjoy quiet country roads from the seaside town of Nairn and visit a 16th century tower house

Start/finish Nairn harbour
Distance 19 miles
Surface Minor roads, short tarmac cycle track section, main road crossing
Map OS Landranger 27

If lounging about on one of Nairn's beautiful beaches isn't enough for you, this spin out to a historic castle will soon blow the sand off your feet.

The minor roads around here are generally very quiet, even in the height of summer, so cycling on them is a real pleasure.

Starting at the town's harbour, where there's a car park tucked away behind the boats, the ride crosses the River Nairn by the wooden harbour bridge (closed to other traffic). Turn right immediately after the bridge to follow a shared-use riverside path alongside a park.

When you reach another pedestrian bridge, turn left to follow the cycle path across a road beside some new buildings. Turn left onto the road where the cycle path emerges to pass a golf course and leave Nairn behind as the road heads east on the National Cycle Network Route 1.

This delightful stretch goes through Kingsteps before running alongside the remarkable Culbin Forest – where there are an endless number of walks possible. Follow a National Trust for Scotland sign right to Brodie Castle and, just before a level crossing, go left to follow the road into the trees. The 'vehicle

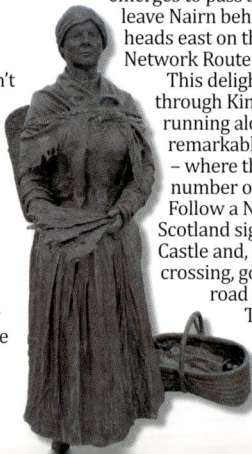

■ Fisherwoman statue at Nairn harbour

entrance' to Brodie Castle is a short distance along this road. The impressive 16th century tower house is full of arts and antiques and the tranquil gardens and grounds offer pleasant short walks.

Back on the bike, turn right opposite the entrance to the castle, and cross a river and the railway before reaching the busy A96 road. Cross this, going right then immediately left, and continue to a T-junction.

Go right then take the first left, signposted to Conicavel and Whitemire. It's the latter village you pass on this ride, which now follows the road up into a forest.

Look out for a right turn on the inside of a long, sweeping right-hand bend. This heads on a narrower road towards Whitemire – instead of continuing towards Whitemire Farm.

Ignore the private road into the village itself and continue to cross the Muckle Burn again before a

sharp right leads gently uphill to a crossroads.

Across the junction is the remains of an ancient ring cairn and it's worth exploring around the stones. There used to be another castle just 100 yards or so up the road from here but nothing remains now – above the ground, at least.

Turn left at the crossroads to enjoy a mile or so of superb downhill before following a sign right towards Auldearn to briefly climb once again. It soon eases then you start to descend a little, ignoring a couple of roads joining from the left.

The route goes left at Newmill, but it's easy to shoot straight past the unmarked junction and end up in Auldearn!

Keep a close eye for a road immediately after crossing a tiny burn, with a row of pretty houses facing you.

Follow it round to Grigorhill and go straight over the B9101 down Granny Barbour's Road into Nairn.

Turn right at the end, then follow the NCN Route 1 sign left through a park to meet the riverside route to the harbour.

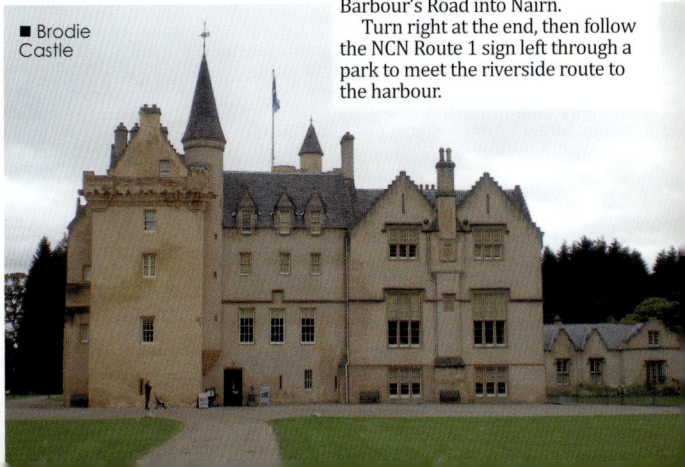

■ Brodie Castle

CYCLE 25

Pit your wits against the epic Bealach na Ba on this challenging tour of the Applecross peninsula

Start/finish Shieldaig
Distance 45 miles
Surface Glorious twisty single-track roads with one major pass and some serious hilly sections to follow
Map OS Landranger 24

■ Refuelling at the Applecross Inn

This ride is guaranteed to take your breath away. If the panoramic views across the sea to Skye and Raasay don't do it, the climb up the Bealach na Ba will.

The pass linking the remote village of Applecross to the rest of the world is a stunning road, twisting and snaking its way up through dramatic Highland mountains to a narrow gap.

It's a serious challenge but, having stood there looking back down those hairpin bends, I can tell you it's worth the effort. And what an effort!

This route does require real stamina, as it has steep climbs from the start to the very end. You also need to be prepared, as the weather can be very different at the 625m (2053ft) bealach, and there are very few opportunities for refreshments along the way.

The friendly Applecross Inn is a great place to break up the ride, however,

and there is the delightfully situated Shieldaig Inn to look forward to at the end. Other than that, you're on your own.

Starting in the pretty coastal village of Shieldaig, head right onto the A896 and head towards Lochcarron, ignoring a sign right to Applecross after a mile – this will be your return route.

After passing Loch Dughaill, your legs soon get a warm up for the real climb ahead, as you climb steadily before dropping down to the Bealach na Ba junction at Tornapress, enjoying views of the Torridon mountains to your left along the beautiful single-track road.

There's a huge sign at the start of the Bealach na Ba road, warning you of the potential perils

■ The warning signs say nothing about cyclists – maybe they should!

ROAD TO APPLECROSS
(BEALACH NA BA)
THIS ROAD RISES TO A HEIGHT OF 2053 Ft.
WITH GRADIENTS OF 1 in 5 AND HAIRPIN BENDS
NOT-ADVISED FOR LEARNER DRIVERS
VERY LARGE VEHICLES OR CARAVANS
AFTER FIRST MILE

ALTERNATIVE LOW LEVEL ROUTE via
Shieldaig - Kenmore - Applecross Road
7½ miles →

■ Looking back down the zig zags from the top of the Bealach na Ba

ahead. Turn right here and head over the River Kishorn on a beautiful stone bridge, then prepare yourself for the big climb.

The route begins fairly gently but gradually gets steeper and steeper – and more and more magnificent – as you work your way towards the summit.

Looking back down the bealach from the top of the series of hairpin bends is an amazing experience, especially when you know you've pedalled your way up there. Expect lots of respect from the patient motorists on the road!

It won't take you long to make the twisty descent into Applecross from the viewpoint, where you can sit and overlook the Cuillins of Skye.

Ignore the campsite sign (unless you want to split the ride up into two days and camp overnight) and continue to the sea front, where a left turn will take you to the inn and the shop.

The route goes right from the seafront junction, rounding the stunning Applecross bay, with its views across the turquoise water to Skye and Raasay, before joining the 'new' road around the peninsula.

It was opened in 1976 – before that, the bealach road was the only ▶

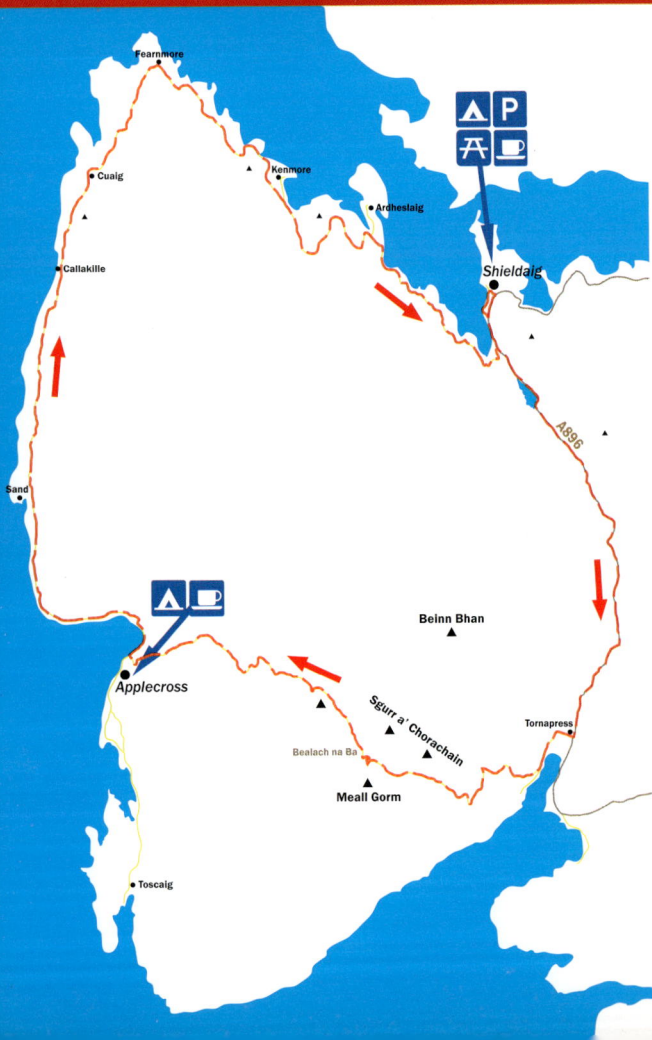

Fearnmore

Kenmore

Cuaig

Ardheslaig

Shieldaig

Callakille

A896

Sand

Beinn Bhan

Applecross

Sgurr a' Chorachain

Tornapress

Bealach na Ba

Meall Gorm

Toscaig

▶ route to the village. But if you expect the hills to be over and done with, you'll be sorely disappointed.

The route is very exposed for the next 10 miles or so and it dips and rises steeply along its way, which can be tough going, especially if you're riding into a headwind.

There's a car park near the 93m trig point, from which views east to Beinn Alligin and Liathach inspire you onwards.

To your left, you can follow your progress up the length of Raasay and Rona, visible along the sound all the way up to Fearnmore at the north-west tip of the Applecross peninsula.

Here, the road turns south-east and, believe it or not, becomes even more hilly! As well as the ups, however, there are some incredible downs – particularly the descent into Ardheslaig around an exposed crag.

Shortly, the road passes a bright white house with a red roof and you get your first glimpse of Shieldaig for some time.

You'll not be surprised to hear there are more hills before you reach the junction with the A896 again and turn left back to the village.

The final flat mile is a rare treat and, turning left into Shieldaig, the village makes the perfect setting to finish this challenging but truly spectacular ride.

■ A glimpse of Shieldaig across the water is a welcome sight from the new road

CHECKLIST WALKS

Tick	Date	Route
☐		1 - Carn na Leitire
☐		2 - Inverfarigaig to Foyers
☐		3 - From firth to fort
☐		4 - Cromarty Sutors
☐		5 - Plodda and Home Falls
☐		6 - Dunain Hill
☐		7 - Reelig Glen tall trees
☐		8 - Ben Wyvis epic
☐		9 - South Loch Ness
☐		10 - Tomich monument
☐		11 - Allt na Criche and beyond
☐		12 - Skye circular
☐		13 - Knockfarrel
☐		14 - Culloden's bloody moor
☐		15 - Meall Fuar-mhonaidh
☐		16 - Tour of Inverness
☐		17 - Beinn a' Bha'ach Ard
☐		18 - Black Isle railway
☐		19 - Drumnadrochit woods
☐		20 - Beinn Eighe Mountain Trail
☐		21 - Beauly riverside
☐		22 - An Torr, Dores
☐		23 - Loch Affric
☐		24 - Black Rock Gorge
☐		25 - Carrbridge explorer

CHECKLIST CYCLES

Tick	Date	Route
☐		1 - Across the Monadhliath
☐		2 - Strathpeffer natural trails
☐		3 - March to Dulsie Bridge
☐		4 - Kilmuir
☐		5 - Loch Ness monster
☐		6 - Tornagrain link
☐		7 - Gaick and Drumochter
☐		8 - Abriachan tester
☐		9 - A tour of the Black Isle
☐		10 - Loch Ruthven
☐		11 - Glen Coiltie
☐		12 - Wade's road escape
☐		13 - Around the Beauly Firth
☐		14 - Glen Affric off-roader
☐		15 - Three bridges
☐		16 - The Aird cycle route
☐		17 - Across Ross
☐		18 - Clava Cairns & Fort George
☐		19 - Ross-shire round
☐		20 - Corrieyairack Pass
☐		21 - Lairg to Durness
☐		22 - NCN Route 1 to Tain
☐		23 - Strathglass & Culnakirk
☐		24 - Nairn to Brodie Castle
☐		25 - Applecross adventure

Note of thanks

This book has involved a lot of hard work – and even more fun – over a period of around 18 months.

I'd like to say a huge thank you to everyone who has helped me pull it together, from those who joined me on the routes to the people who have guided me through the publishing maze so I could share these fantastic routes with you all.

A special big thanks to my wife Meg for sharing so many of these adventures with me and helping me get the work finished on time. I couldn't have done it without you.

I'd like to hear your thoughts on the routes published here – get in touch via my website BL6.co.uk (QR opposite) or contact me on Twitter @BL6John.

I hope you enjoy these outings as much as I have. Stay safe and have fun.

John Davidson

■ Broch below Ben Hope, Sutherland

KNOW THE CODE BEFORE YOU GO

SCOTTISH OUTDOOR ACCESS CODE   outdooraccess-scotland.com